Designing Purpose-Built Drones for Ardupilot Pixhawk 2.1

Build drones with Ardupilot

Ty Audronis

BIRMINGHAM - MUMBAI

Designing Purpose-Built Drones for Ardupilot Pixhawk 2.1

Copyright © 2017 Packt Publishing

First published: December 2017

Production reference: 1271217

Published by Packt Publishing Ltd.
Livery Place
35 Livery Street
Birmingham
B3 2PB, UK.
ISBN 978-1-78646-916-8

www.packtpub.com

Credits

Author
Ty Audronis

Reviewer
Ayan Pahwa
Ersin Gonul

Commissioning Editor
Kartikey Pandey

Acquisition Editor
Prachi Bisht

Content Development Editor
Dattatraya More

Technical Editor
Sneha Hanchate

Copy Editor
Laxmi Subramanian

Project Coordinator
Shweta H Birwatkar

Proofreader
Safis Editing

Indexer
Aishwarya Gangawane

Graphics
Tania Dutta

Production Coordinator
Melywn Dsa

About the Author

Ty Audronis has been called "a technology-age renaissance man." He's a professional drone pilot, post-production specialist in the entertainment and media industries, a highly experienced interactive game developer, and an accomplished digital artist. He has worked for companies ranging from frog Design to California Academy of Sciences in roles, where he has worn many hats.

Ty has been programming software and games since 1981 (when he was 8 years old) professionally. He majored in "Computer Generated Animation and Visual Effects" in college (where he won "Best Animation" for the entire CSU system – a Rosebud Award). He has been building drones since the days when sensors and components had to be torn out of cell phones and game controllers.

Ty is also a mentor, having taught many interns his skills and speaks regularly at venues, including Interdrone. He also serves on the advisory board for the Society of Aerial Cinematographers and for Genarts (now Boris) Sapphire.

About the Reviewer

Ayan Pahwa is an embedded software engineer from New Delhi, India currently working at Mentor Graphics - a Siemens business with 5 plus years of experience in building and racing first person view multi-rotor drones. His professional work areas mainly focus on embedded firmware, device drivers, automotive IoT, and Linux system programming. He has co-founded SDIoT for flourishing drone and other new technologies within local communities. His drone aerial videos can be viewed on his YouTube channel.

Ersin Gonul is a senior design engineer at Turkish Aerospace Industries in Ankara, Turkey. Previously Gonul worked as R & D engineer for companies which they develop unmanned aerial vehicles. He graduated with honors from Selcuk University in Electrical and Electronics Engineering and also he holds a Master degree of Electrical and Electronics Engineering from the Hacettepe University, Ankara. His expertise based on helicopter autopilots and unmanned systems. He is passionate about aviation, multicopters, VTOLs and their control systems. He also holds a Private Pilot License (PPL-H).

www.PacktPub.com

For support files and downloads related to your book, please visit www.PacktPub.com. Did you know that Packt offers eBook versions of every book published, with PDF and ePub files available? You can upgrade to the eBook version at www.PacktPub.comand as a print book customer, you are entitled to a discount on the eBook copy. Get in touch with us at service@packtpub.com for more details. At www.PacktPub.com, you can also read a collection of free technical articles, sign up for a range of free newsletters and receive exclusive discounts and offers on Packt books and eBooks.

https://www.packtpub.com/mapt

Get the most in-demand software skills with Mapt. Mapt gives you full access to all Packt books and video courses, as well as industry-leading tools to help you plan your personal development and advance your career.

Why subscribe?

- Fully searchable across every book published by Packt
- Copy and paste, print, and bookmark content
- On demand and accessible via a web browser

Customer Feedback

Thanks for purchasing this Packt book. At Packt, quality is at the heart of our editorial process. To help us improve, please leave us an honest review on this book's Amazon page at https://www.amazon.com/dp/1786469162.

If you'd like to join our team of regular reviewers, you can email us at customerreviews@packtpub.com. We award our regular reviewers with free eBooks and videos in exchange for their valuable feedback. Help us be relentless in improving our products.

Table of Contents

Preface

We live in the drone age. Drones currently serve purposes in defense, entertainment, and in some countries, package delivery. However, the drone age is still in its infancy. There are a plethora of uses for drones that are just on the cusp of being discovered; drones for mapping, drones for convenience, and even drones for scientific research.

This book will walk you through the design process for drones that navigate the air, land, and even the sea. We will show you how to come up with ideas, overcome the limitations of budget and current technology, and implement them. However, a drone without a "brain" is just an RC vehicle. We'll show you how to integrate the Pixhawk 2.1 guidance system into your drone and how to add peripherals and sensors to Pixhawk to make ordinary RC vehicles into smart drones that serve purposes.

What this book covers

Chapter 1, *Drones 101*, introduces you to the world of drones and explains that there are many types of drones. We also give you a high-level overview of Ardupilot and Pixhawk flight controller systems. Finally, we walk you through some of the safety best practices to minimize the risks associated with prototyping new drones.

Chapter 2, *Your First Drone - An Autonomous RC Car*, walks you through kitbashing (using an existing) RC car and turning it into a surface drone (a rover). We show you the basics of designing, 3D-printing, and even molding new parts for your rover to adapt it to Pixhawk. You will be given even more familiarity with the plugs on the Pixhawk 2.1 board and how sensors are attached, as well as a basic overview of the Mission Planner interface. By the end of this chapter, you will have an understanding of how to create a rover using Pixhawk 2.1, a GPS sensor, and a remote telemetry transmitter.

Chapter 3, *A Drone for Hunters – Autonomous Duck Decoy*, takes the principles of a rover and applies them to the open water. This chapter focuses largely on the process of coming up with a marketable idea and planning your design. You will be shown how to cannibalize parts from an RC boat and implement them into a custom 3D-printed hull (a duck). We will also educate you on the pitfalls of a water drone with regards to waterproofing, ballast, and even water-cooling your drive motor.

Chapter 4, *A Drone for Golfers*, takes purpose-built rovers to the next level by showing you that drones can fit into almost any market demographic: in this case, golf. We will build a golf trolley on an existing RC golf trolley's frame and motor system. It implements skid-steering and Bluetooth for telemetry and control, enabling it to follow a golfer that is carrying a phone in their pocket. Also, we will integrate a new sensor: a LIDAR rangefinder that allows the trolley to avoid obstacles while it follows the golfer autonomously.

Chapter 5, *Introduction to UAVs*, transitions the reader from the surface to the air. Aerial drones represent a whole new level of complexity. With weight considerations, balance, and safety concerns being the focus of this chapter, you will learn to think more like an aeronautical engineer when designing your aerial drones.

Chapter 6, A Simple Multicopter Drone, shows the reader how to build and tune a multicopter drone. We adopt a "GoPro" gimbal (designed to stabilize a GoPro camera) to hold a 360° VR camera (a Ricoh Theta S). We also walk you step-by-step through the Mission Planner interface to get a ground station up and running, which will display a video on a laptop screen, along with the heads-up display and even allows you to fly the drone using gaming joysticks.

Chapter 7, The Holy Grail - A Fixed Wing Drone, walks you through designing and setting up a fixed-wing drone. We will integrate an airspeed sensor (pitot tube) and use a rangefinder again but this time to sense altitude from the ground to assist with autonomous landings. This chapter largely focuses on the Mission Planner software. Using it to tune a fixed-wing drone to fly properly, we will execute autonomous missions and even land with no input from the pilot.

Chapter 8, *The Principles of VTOL with Pixhawk*, is a bonus chapter added due to the popular demand from the drone community. VTOL (Vertical Takeoff and Landing) drones are airplanes that can also hover and land/take off like a helicopter. Rather than build a drone in this chapter, we walk you through the concepts of planning, building, and tuning a VTOL aircraft.

Chapter 9, *Programming Ardupilot*, is largely a reference chapter designed to give you quick reference to the Mission Planner interface and all of the basic parameters therein.

What you need for this book

This book guides you through building various types of drones by example. You do not have to buy all of the materials, nor even build along-side. All this book really requires from you is an imagination, which we hope to spark by example.

Who this book is for

This book is intended beginners and intermediate drone enthusiasts. But at some point, even professional designers may benefit from the book's contents.

Conventions

In this book, you will find a number of text styles that distinguish between different kinds of information. Here are some examples of these styles and an explanation of their meaning.

Code words in text, database table names, folder names, filenames, file extensions, pathnames, dummy URLs, user input, and Twitter handles are shown as follows: "The next lines of code read the link and assigns it to the to the `BeautifulSoup` function."

New terms and **important words** are shown in bold. Words that you see on the screen, for example, in menus or dialog boxes, appear in the text like this: "In order to download new modules, we will go to **Files** | **Settings** | **Project Name** | **Project Interpreter**."

 Warnings or important notes appear in a box like this.

 Tips and tricks appear like this.

Reader feedback

Feedback from our readers is always welcome. Let us know what you think about this book-what you liked or disliked. Reader feedback is important for us as it helps us develop titles that you will really get the most out of. To send us general feedback, simply email `feedback@packtpub.com`, and mention the book's title in the subject of your message. If there is a topic that you have expertise in and you are interested in either writing or contributing to a book, see our author guide at `www.packtpub.com/authors`.

Customer support

Now that you are the proud owner of a Packt book, we have a number of things to help you to get the most from your purchase.

Downloading the color images of this book

We also provide you with a PDF file that has color images of the screenshots/diagrams used in this book. The color images will help you better understand the changes in the output. You can download this file from `https://www.packtpub.com/sites/default/files/downloads/DesigningPurposeBuiltDronesforArdupilotPixhawk21_ColorImages.pdf`.

Errata

Although we have taken every care to ensure the accuracy of our content, mistakes do happen. If you find a mistake in one of our books-maybe a mistake in the text or the code-we would be grateful if you could report this to us. By doing so, you can save other readers from frustration and help us improve subsequent versions of this book. If you find any errata, please report them by visiting `http://www.packtpub.com/submit-errata`, selecting your book, clicking on the **Errata Submission Form** link, and entering the details of your errata. Once your errata are verified, your submission will be accepted and the errata will be uploaded to our website or added to any list of existing errata under the Errata section of that title.

To view the previously submitted errata, go to `https://www.packtpub.com/books/content/support` and enter the name of the book in the search field. The required information will appear under the **Errata** section.

Piracy

Piracy of copyrighted material on the internet is an ongoing problem across all media. At Packt, we take the protection of our copyright and licenses very seriously. If you come across any illegal copies of our works in any form on the internet, please provide us with the location address or website name immediately so that we can pursue a remedy.

Please contact us at `copyright@packtpub.com` with a link to the suspected pirated material.

We appreciate your help in protecting our authors and our ability to bring you valuable content.

Questions

If you have a problem with any aspect of this book, you can contact us at `questions@packtpub.com`, and we will do our best to address the problem.

1
Drones 101

Congratulations! You've taken the first step into the exciting world of designing and developing your very own purpose-built drone. Humankind has constantly been pushing the edges of their technology. Our technological progression is built into our DNA so thoroughly that we mark complete eras of our history with the technological state of the art. The Bronze Age, the Industrial Era, Space-Age, Information Age, and now the "Drone Era." It truly is exciting to live in the drone era. Well, we have a lot to cover, so let's get started:

We'll be covering the following topics in this chapter:

- Introduction to drones
- Purposes for drones
- Types of drones
- Ardupilot 101
- Safety and best practices

Introduction to drones

What is a drone? Twenty years ago, the answer was easy. Ignoring the definitions having to do with insects, a drone was a term strictly used for a military autonomous flying vehicle. Drones were (mostly) used for target practice or for gathering intelligence (reconnaissance). Along came a company called **Dragan** that made one of the first commercially available quadrocopters (the **DraganFlyer**) and the term **Quad Helicopter** was born.

Their first commercially available multicopter was simply called the **Quad Helicopter** and came out in 1997 (it is shown in the following image):

The original DraganFlyer Quad Helicopter (1997). Picture courtesy of DraganFlyer

In the 2000s, the term *drone* became synonymous with military strikes. Between the United States Presidents Bush and Obama, the United States racked up many attacks on targets with connections to terrorism. So, the term "drone" had an ominous implication.

In 2010, Parrot came out with a multicopter that implemented **augmented reality** (**AR**) on a cell phone. This game allowed players to shoot down each other's real-life multicopters. The multicopter was titled the **AR Drone** (probably as a marketing attempt to capitalize on the ominous nature of the term drone). Really, it was the first multicopter you could buy in your local shopping mall and plaza (it was available at all Sharper Image stores). The public finally had its first look at multicopters. There it was—Drone stamped in all-caps on the front of the box.

Who could resist? I had spent days, weeks, years (even) building drones by tearing apart other electronics to get accelerometers, GPS modules, and other components to build my own drone. Could it really be so easy that all I had to do was go down to the mall and buy one? Yes. The following image shows me in 2010 testing out an AR Drone bought from Sharper Image:

Testing an AR Drone (1.0) in 2010 from "Sharper Image" (Pacifica, CA)

In 2011, the glory of military drones got a big stain. It turned out that these surgical drone strikes were sometimes taking out civilians, US citizens in foreign countries, and missing terrorists all together. Suddenly the term drone was becoming something that the general public associated with fear and even rage. Protests ensued (as shown in the following image):

Creative Commons Picture by: Fibonacci Blue

Soon, turnkey systems (like the DJI Phantom) were available with cameras already installed and sold at big-box retailers. This led to privacy concerns from opponents to the craft. They had been handed a new term for multicopters on a silver platter, a term that struck fear and loathing into the hearts of people all around the planet. A term even synonymous with murder-drone. In the following image, you can see the first in the line of DJI Phantom drones:

The DJI Phantom (version 1) - The first of the most popular drone line ever created. Those three prongs on the center of the hull are a mount for a GoPro camera

The multicopter community resisted the term *drone* with all its might. People were in hysterics. In Santa Rosa, California (2013), a police officer even confiscated a property owner's drone. He was flying it over his own vineyards and posting the videos on YouTube. The police officer stated that it would be a matter of months before you saw *fly by shootings*. The police department had no legal standing and was forced to return the Phantom.

Legislators around the country were making local laws against drones. In Los Angeles (the area that hosts Hollywood and the bulk of the aerial cinematography industry), drones were outlawed. (Later these laws would be overturned as the FAA finally stepped in and stated that local and state governments had no jurisdiction over airspace.) At the time, it looked as if drones may just go the way of the condor. But then something wonderful happened.

The industry stopped resisting the term drone. I remember on my first drone book with Packt, *Building Multicopter Video Drones*, resisting the word *drone* in the title. But they convinced me it would be good for search engine food. As we (in the industry) stopped resisting the term and started educating the public about the safety, best practices, and usefulness of drones the negative implications lost all meaning. And (as in the following image), drones even took on an entirely new meaning:

A group of drone pilots from "Humanitarian Drones" and FEMA team members assisting in Port Arthur, TX during Hurricane Harvey relief efforts. Photo by Daniel Herbert (of Humanitarian Drones)

Suddenly, drones were saving lives (with search and rescue), helping people recover from disasters (with assessment of damage, as shown in the following image), and responsible for great shots in feature films and people's favourite documentaries. Then, something completely weird happened:

A DJI Inspire 2 conducting damage assessment and mapping in the aftermath of Hurricane Harvey in Houston, Texas. Photo taken by Brian Scott of Humanitarian Drones

Drones were no longer multicopters. The term covered anything that flew under remote control. This happened with the FAA's **small Unmanned Aerial System (sUAS)** rules. The media dubbed these rules *drone legislation*. Suddenly, drones had wings, even jet engines. Now, they didn't even have to fly autonomously, the radio-controlled airplane that grandpa flew on weekends was a drone.

Then, it went further. The guidance systems used in multicopter drones were being repurposed to control ground vehicles (rovers) and water vehicles (boats and submersibles). Now, in 2017, you actually hear companies coming out with *underwater drones*.

In short, the answer to the original question, "What (exactly) is a drone?" is simply a robot-a vehicle of any type that is either not controlled by a human (autonomous) or controlled by a human via remote control. It may not be the Oxford English Dictionary's definition, but it is the definition that the common public accepts when they hear the word drone.

And, as for the proof that we're living in the Drone Era? In the height of the space age (the mid-1980s), men on rocket packs flew into stadiums for the opening ceremonies for the 1984 Olympics, and even during the Super Bowl XIX half-time show. Now, we have drone-shows for those same venues. Of course, we still have a ways to go for full-tilt drone acceptance. After all, the drone part of the half-time show had to be filmed days earlier for fear of a drone attack during the show, or at least fear of mass hysteria in the venue. But we'll take it.

Purposes for drones

Drones are just for taking pictures, right? Wrong! Drones can be useful for just about anything and everything. Here are just a few examples:

- Suffering in a drought (hello, California) but need to water your crops? You can use a drone to map your whole farm. Then, run analysis on crop health, so that you know where to direct water. All the while sipping iced tea on your porch.
- Want to walk the golf course, but don't want to hire a caddy or carry your own clubs? Caddy drone to the rescue! Make a motorized golf trolley, and have it follow the GPS signal on your cell phone as your walk the golf course.
- Maybe you're a herpetologist on an expedition to a remote location and you found a new species of tree frog. Get it back to base-camp from miles away in an autonomous powered glider. Just load the frog into the payload bay, give it a toss above the treeline and let it fly (and land at) home! Then, just wait for base camp to get the specimen and send the powered glider back to you for your expedition to continue.
- You're a lifeguard at a beach and see someone having trouble. Launch an aerial drone that drops a boat-drone to tow the person back to shore. All the while, you don't have to leave your station (leaving the rest of the beach-goers without a lifeguard). You can meet the victim at the beach with medical supplies you may need and you're not too exhausted to help out!

The list goes on and on and on. If you can think of something requiring delivery of an item, manual labour requiring movement to another location, or just something to save time, a purpose for a drone will be found. The possibilities are quite literally limitless.

The following image shows the (Israeli Defense Force) *Air Mule*. It is an autonomous ambulance drone designed to go into the battlefield and airlift wounded soldiers and civilians back to a medical facility at over 100 miles per hour, all with no pilot onboard:

There is some fear that drones will eventually replace people on certain jobs. This fear is slowly being realized with autonomous cars (as UBER is talking about rolling out). After all, these are drones too. However, I prefer to think of it as freeing people from the mundane tasks in favour of the pursuit of their imaginations (like figuring out more uses for drones). Besides, people are still needed to maintain drones, monitor them, and analyse the data they provide. (At least until **artificial intelligence (AI)** is better at abstracting ideas and problem solving.)

It goes even further than a single drone for a single purpose though. With *swarming*, multiple drones can specialize in parts of a task and cooperate to achieve a very complicated result. For instance:

- Geologists deploying swarms of aerial drones to get infra-red imagery of fault lines while additional swarms of rovers (with seismic sensors) can monitor those fault lines for activity. That sort of purpose can save thousands of lives.
- Swarms of submersible micro-drones in the oceans can monitor currents and track tidal-waves headed toward land. They could even be powered using the kinetic energy of the currents to generate their electricity. People could be evacuated in time to save them.
- In the event of a natural disaster, electricity (and therefore communications) is the cause of many casualties. A swarm of communication drones (cell tower repeater replacements) can fan out across a country to re-establish the communication networks in a matter of minutes.

These are certainly some altruistic and noble uses for swarming, but the military also sees the benefit of drone swarms. The following image shows a recent test of drone swarms (deployed by dropping them from a pair of f-18 Hornets) used to map out a battle-field in real-time for mission commanders and soldiers on the ground:

Drone swarms can also be used by the entertainment industry to cover sporting events, if one drone is running low on batteries, another takes off to take its place. Drone swarms could be deployed over golf courses to help enthusiasts find their ill-hit balls that have gone off into the weeds. Farmers could use drone swarms to monitor crops, plant seeds, monitor watering patterns (and waste from evaporating water, or atomized sprinklers going into the air).

Again, the uses for drones are limitless.

We could list potential uses for drones all day, all night, every day, and every year, for our lifetimes. So, how do we realize this potential?

Well, to figure out how to make drones, we'll always first start off with how to implement existing tech and components to make what we want. The first step is to think in terms of what types of drones exist currently.

Types of drones

Drones come in two categories with several subcategories. There are surface/subsurface drones, and aerial drones. Let's dive further into each.

USV drones

USV simply stands for either **Unmanned Surface Vehicle** or **Unmanned Submersible Vehicle**. The same acronym of **USV** is used for both. These types of drones are usually referred to as *Rovers* or *Submersibles* respectively.

Rovers

Rovers usually either have treads (like a tank) or wheels (like a car). The *Mars Rovers* are great examples of USV Rovers. They move along the surface of Mars taking various readings and measurements in an effort to explore the surface of another planet without the risk to human life. The following picture shows one of these Mars Rovers:

Not every endeavor for a rover needs to be quite so lofty as to explore another planet. Rovers are currently used in aspects of our daily lives (the iRobot Roomba is a daily life example of a USV Rover) all the way through exploring our own planet (rovers designed to explore lava flows—areas far too dangerous and inhospitable to humans).

However, rovers don't have to simply be driven across the ground. Some rovers are actually boats designed to skid across the surface of water for various purposes. An example of boat-drone USV is the one designed by the US Navy to escort ships through pirate-ridden waters, and protect naval vessels from other hostile vessels in dangerous waters (eliminating, or at least reducing, the need for bloated battle-groups).

In this book, we will be designing three surface rovers:

- A basic autonomous RC car which serves no purpose other than your education on the basics of implementing the Ardupilot interface.
- A water USV that serves the purpose of a duck decoy which autonomously navigates pre-planned routes around a pond for hunters. Hmm... one wonders what that might go for in a store?
- A ground USV golf caddy. This will show you how to make a rover follow a GPS tracker (in the form of the user's cell phone). This caddy is designed to move your clubs around the golf course without having to carry your bag, nor even tell the caddy where to go. It will simply follow you.

Submersibles

Submersibles are vehicles designed to go beneath the surface of a liquid. Traditionally, this liquid is water. However, submersible vehicles could potentially be used to monitor other liquids, such as fermentation tanks at breweries, mixing tanks at chemical plants, and diving into raw sewage tanks. Other than diving into a vat of beer, I'm sure you can see how using drones is preferable to diving in yourself.

We won't be attempting to create a submersible in this book. However, the techniques employed are very similar to the subject matter of this book. Submersibles should only be attempted by highly experienced drone designers, as they'll have to contend with reduced ability to utilize GPS, reduced radio transmission distance, and highly reduced visibility in water (or other liquids). Therefore, technologies such as **forward looking infrared** (**FLIR**), signal repeaters, and collision avoidance (via SONAR) should be considered. However, as you can see from the following image, the similarities between underwater drones and fixed-wing aerial drones (airplanes) are fairly obvious:

The similarities between the Navy's "Ocean Glider" submersible drone and the original X-1 airplane (the airplane which first broke the sound-barrier) are rather astounding.

UAV drones

UAV stands for **Unmanned Aerial Vehicle**. Simply stated, this is any drone that flies. However, much like the term USV can also include submersibles, this category can also cover vehicles that go into space (such as the Pioneer satellites, the Cassini probe, or even the Air Force's replacement for the Space Shuttle—the X37B.

The US Air Force's X37b can be drop-launched from a high-flying airplane, or mounted to a rocket. It can also autonomously stay in space for several years, change orbital paths, and return to the ground for an autonomous landing. The actual payloads and missions are classified. You didn't really think we'd rely on Russia and civilian agencies for all the United States' needs in space, did you?

We won't bother to get into space any further. After all, if you're working for NASA you probably don't need this book. Still, it was cool to mention. In the air, UAVs can be broken into five essential categories:

Multirotors

Sometimes, people refer to these as *quadcopters* or *quadrocopters*. Technically, this isn't accurate unless the multirotor has four-propellers. There are also hexacopters (six-propellers), octacopters, (eight-propellers), and even all the way up to thirty-two-propellers (although I have no idea what that word would even be). So, you can see how multirotor simplifies it all. After all, they are essentially the same type of aircraft, just with more or less motors and propellers. (It's like calling a monofoil and a biplane an airplane, but calling a monofoil a *biplane* is incorrect).

How do multicopters fly?

The principle is simple. So simple (in fact) that you may wonder why these weren't a thing until recently. Propellers blow air down to provide lift and the airframe (the whole body) tilts to direct that thrust behind (to go forward), in front (to go backward), or to either side (to slide left or right). You can see this in the following illustration:

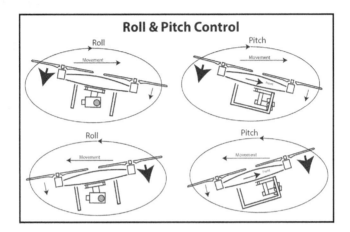

But then there's controlling it.

It requires thousands of calculations per second to decide exactly how much power should go to each motor to keep the aircraft level and stable in the air. No two motors come out exactly the same. So, it's not just a matter of providing equal voltage to each motor. It's a matter of adjusting that voltage to each motor based on what's currently happening to the aircraft. So, in essence the aircraft doesn't fly it reacts to its inability to fly and compensates for it. And then there's turning (yaw).

You may notice there's no tail rotor on a multicopter. Tail rotors on traditional helicopters serve two functions:

- Keep the airframe (the body) of the aircraft from spinning out of control. After all, Newtonian Physics tells us that for every action, there is an equal and opposite reaction. If the motor is turning the primary rotor, what's to stop it from spinning the body in the opposite direction?
- By varying the pitch of the blades on the tail rotor, more or less thrust (as well as the direction of the thrust) can be controlled. This lets the pilot yaw the aircraft (turn it).

So, how does a multirotor achieve yaw? The answer is in the preceding first reason. There are (usually) even numbers of rotors on a multicopter. Half of these rotors spin in one direction (clockwise) and the other half in the other direction (anti-clockwise). When you want to turn left, the blades spinning to the right speed up and the blades spinning to the left slow down. This way, the effective lift remains the same but the torque from the motors yaws the aircraft to the left. The opposite happens when turning to the right. The following illustration shows this in action:

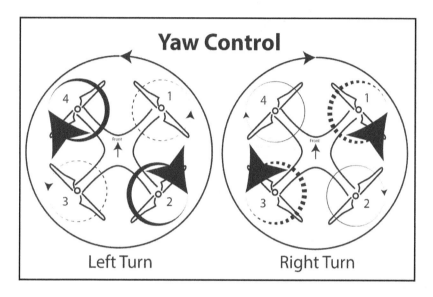

This is also why tricopters (three rotors) are largely not used. They were notoriously unstable and battery-inefficient. They looked super cool though. Rather like the drop ship from the movie *Aliens*. However, a variation of the hexacopter (six-rotors) uses that motif (which brings us to yet another variation on blade-configuration). A flat-hexacopter has all-six blades stationed on a single plane. The over-under version of a hexacopter looks like a tricopter with three basic lift points, but counter-rotating blades stacked atop one another so one plane of blades moves in one direction; while the one following moves opposite.

The following picture shows a standard quadcopter (upper left), an over-under hexacopter (upper-right), and a flat-hexacopter (bottom). Most configurations for multicopters are now flat, as it's more efficient for battery time and lift capabilities:

So, as you can see, multicopters are a platform based on a simple principle that is extremely complicated to make work. You (the pilot) don't actually fly a multicopter. It flies itself. Instead, you really just tell it where to go and what to do. You don't pilot a multicopter, you wrangle it.

For the guidance system (in our case we'll be using Pixhawk 2.1—an Ardupilot-based system) to accurately calculate what each motor should be doing there is a plethora of sensors it needs:

- **Accelerometers**: Measure the attitude of the aircraft to see whether it's level, what direction it's moving in (relative to last attitude). These essentially measure the linear velocity. So, there need to be several of these sensors in order to measure all axis of movement. The Pixhawk has three accelerometers which are quite good and very fast. However, more can be added.
- **Gyroscopes**: These differ from accelerometers in that they sense angular movement (roll, pitch, and yaw). Each gyroscope measures one axis of movement, so three are needed. Pixhawk includes three gyros.

- **Magnetometers**: This sensor functions essentially as a compass. They measure the Earth's magnetic field and can tell the vehicle's relative heading to north. However, as aircraft can roll and pitch, one should be implemented for each axis and compared to each other (as one magnetometer may get locked if perpendicular to north). Pixhawk has three of these.
- **Barometers**: A barometer measures air pressure. Because air pressure changes at various altitudes, this method can tell the relative altitude to the takeoff point. Amazingly, these can be quite accurate (down to individual inches) depending on the number of sensors, and their sensitivity. Pixhawk has two built in.
- **Global positioning system (GPS)**: GPS tells the Pixhawk where it is (on the planet). We'll get deeper into GPS and how it works in a later chapter, but let's just say that not all GPS receivers are created equally. GPS is an approximation and various factors determine how accurate it is. GPS is not included with Pixhawk. You must buy your own GPS module for it.

So, accuracy of sensors is extremely important (as you can see) with regard to flying multicopters. If it's truly flying itself and you're just telling it where to go, you want that robot brain to have as much information (which is as accurate) as possible.

The myth with multicopters is that they're extremely simple. This is probably because they are fairly easy to fly. That myth should be dispelled right here and now. Of all the drone-types, they are the most difficult to design and build. You'll find that parts should work together, but don't. You'll find that balancing lift to flight-time is extremely difficult. And you'll find that when things go wrong, they go very wrong. Trust me I have the scars to prove it. So, when we get into multicopters, please pay the utmost attention to safety. They are essentially flying Cuisinarts.

Fixed-wing drones – airplanes

Airplanes are considered by many as the *Holy Grail* of UAVs. They can generally fly for a lot longer than multicopters (as they have wings and don't have to use up battery power on lift). They are much easier to fly (as they can actually glide and, if the motor cuts out, they don't drop like a rock). However, the difficulty with airplanes is takeoff and landing.

Since airplanes don't hover, they must be moving at speed to take off and land. Landing an airplane isn't too easy either. They must touch the ground softly, or they may bounce up again, stall, and crash. So, how do you design a drone to land at speed softly? It's not easy. But Pixhawk has been known to do this pretty well.

Also, since an airplane needs to maintain a certain speed in the air to keep wind flowing over the wings in order to provide lift (called **air speed**); the guidance system needs to know how fast it's moving through the air (not just in relation to the ground). In addition to all of the sensors employed by the Pixhawk for a multicopter; one more sensor is needed for an airplane a pitot tube.

You'll find a pitot tube on any real airplane to measure airspeed. This device is the little *sticks* you see protruding from the sides or nose of the airplane. The following image shows how a pitot tube works:

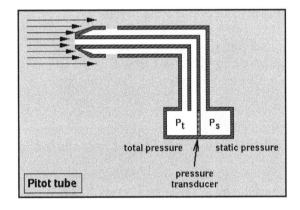

Image courtesy of Wikimedia commons

The following image shows a pitot tube on a piloted aircraft:

The Pixhawk does not have this sensor, but one can be purchased to use with it.

Fixed-wing drones can also be launched in a variety of ways. Some are thrown; others are launched on catapult systems, while still others are launched by taking off like traditional aircraft (rolling takeoff with wheels).

The following image shows one of my drones (2012) being launched via a catapult system known as a **Jetapult**:

Since this drone had a seven-foot wingspan, it was far too large to launch by throwing it. The system was very simple. It used PVC pipe to angle the aircraft and slide it up at a slight angle while a bungie cord pulled the aircraft forward at a high rate of acceleration. If you look closely, you can see the black bungie cord wadded up on the ground just behind the (now flying) drone. The release was a simple foot-pedal that slid a ring off a peg.

Although this is a simple mechanism, even military drones are sometimes launched from catapults (as shown in the following image):

Hybrid drones – VTOL

You may wonder why we spent so much time on takeoff and landing. **Vertical Takeoff and/or Landing (VTOL)** drones solve a lot of issues, but present a high degree of complexity. These drones can take off like a helicopter (or multicopter), fly like an airplane, and land again like a helicopter/multicopter.

The XplusOne (by Xcraft) takes off and can even fly like a quadcopter, but then it can transition into forward flight like an airplane. As you can see though, designing such an aircraft is incredibly difficult. Wind resistance from the wing (when vertical) can create instability during multirotor flight and transitioning to airplane flight can be equally difficult. However, the most difficult proposition of all is coming back to quad-flight for landing. How do you keep the aircraft from ballooning (gaining altitude) and then stalling into a crash? You should only attempt this when you have a high degree of funding and experience, because it's virtually guaranteed that you'll crash it several times before tuning your design to be just right.

Helicopter drones

Traditional helicopters do have some advantages. They can fly faster than multicopters (usually) and are more stable during forward flight (due to a tail fin and horizontal fins). They can also (sometimes) stay in the air longer, as they do not require the quick responsiveness of electric motors. Therefore, they can fly using combustion engines or even turbo-shaft engines, meaning they can carry more fuel and fly for longer. The following picture shows a US Navy helicopter drone:

However, traditional helicopters shift the pitch of their blades through the use of a *swash plate*. They also (usually) shift the pitch of their tail rotor blades using a similar method (albeit less complicated). A swash plate is basically two plates that rotate and move up and down the rotor shaft to alter the pitch of the blades. How does a helicopter tilt forward to start moving? The swash plate tilts and shafts going down to the swash plate make the blades bite into the air more at the back of the helicopter, and bite less toward the front (producing more downforce at the rear and less at the front).

All of these moving mechanical parts require lubing and maintenance between every flight. The more complex a machine is, the more opportunity there is for failure. So, although there are advantages to traditional helicopters the disadvantages (in terms of cost and maintenance schedule) make them a nonstarter for many.

The following image shows how a swash plate works. The red disk remains stationary and rotates or moves up and down. Meanwhile, the beige parts turn with the rotor head and the aqua control rods shift the pitch of the blades depending on where they are positioned during their rotation cycle:

That's the end of helicopters for the purposes of this book. As there really is little difference between helicopters and multicopters for the purposes of our Pixhawk, we have chosen to cover multicopters in this book.

Dirigible drones – Blimps

Blimps are actually pretty great. They can stay aloft for extremely extended periods of time. They are very stable as well. However, they can be a bit of an eyesore to landscapes as they have to be quite large to carry any sort of payload. The following image shows a Navy dirigible drone:

There are some other drawbacks to dirigible drones. They must be inflated, costing large amounts of money each time you fly in whatever lighter-than-air gas you choose to use (helium, hydrogen, and so on). They are also highly susceptible to strong wind currents (due to their lighter-than-air nature). So, strong engines must be employed to counteract those currents. This adds more weight and therefore more size to the blimp. Due to these limitations and costs, dirigibles are not widely used.

It's a shame, because mechanically, they are the simplest drones to design. It is just that in practice, they are expensive and largely impractical.

Ardupilot 101 – A quick overview of Pixhawk 2.1

The Ardupilot platform (based on the Arduino robotics platform) has been around for a long time. In 2007, it was conceived by a company called 3D Robotics. It's an open code-base (fully programmable), and has exploded in its versatility and capabilities since 2013 with the advent of the Pixhawk line. The latest version (2.1 at the time of the authoring of this book) implements even more versatility and stability through the capabilities of expanding the processing power via the optional Intel Edison Compute Module, and the addition of the cube. The cube contains a triple-redundancy sensor array of gyros, accelerometers, magnetometers, and barometers housed in a cushioned cube-shaped platform designed to minimize vibration and electronic interference.

In addition to Intel Edison, you can use Rasberry Pi, ODroid, NVidia TX1, and BeaglePilot project coprocessors to customize the functionality of your Pixhawk 2.1 in any way you wish. Although not every Pixhawk 2.1 has the Edison port (if you're planning on using Edison, the listing for the Pixhawk you buy should explicitly say *Edison Ready*), the other coprocessors can be added to any Pixhawk board.

Feel overwhelmed? Good. Then the goal is achieved with regard to showing you that the Pixhawk's capabilities are vast. So vast, in fact, that it is a full-on robotics platform brain capable of virtually anything you can imagine. The Pixhawk's limitations are only within the grasp of your programming skills.

Full-disclosure here, we won't be venturing too deeply into the programming languages and commands therein for customizing Pixhawk. That could be a whole book, or rather a series of books, all by itself. Instead, we'll be venturing into Pixhawk as it can be applied to practical purposes in its stock state (with minor tweaks).

The important point is that if DJI represents proprietary systems (although very high quality proprietary systems), Pixhawk represents open architecture. DJI would be like Apple and Pixhawk would be like Linux.

Now, you can breathe. We won't be terrifying and overwhelming you with screens and screens of coding. Let's get into the device itself.

The following image shows the Pixhawk 2.1:

Although, at first glance, the interface for plugs on the device itself looks complicated, you should take a closer look. Each plug type has a unique size and shape with a very clearly written label. We'll get deeper into all of the plugs and whatnot later in the book. But just for the sake of familiarity, let's take a quick look at a few:

- **CAN ports**: Think of a CAN port as a CAN do port. A CAN bus is a common method of communication between devices (such as sensors) and the Pixhawk. You can also daisy-chain these devices. For instance, one device you may want to plug into a CAN port could be a (digital) pitot tube.
- **TELEM ports**: Telem stands for telemetry. These are essentially ports that can send and receive commands and information about exactly what's happening on the Pixhawk. Devices such as coprocessors (except Edison), and **Head's Up Display** (HUD) which overlays information on top of a video feed for transmission to the ground would plug into these ports.
- **ADC ports**: ADC ports are for analog sensors. Analog sensors usually return a voltage (rather than a digital information signal). These are usually used for analog pitot tubes.
- **I2C ports**: Much like the CAN ports, I2C ports can handle many different types of devices via a hub.

- **GPS ports**: This is simply where your GPS sensor plugs in. But why are there two? This has been a request that 3D Robotics listened to from users. Dual GPS can yield a better location sensing. Whichever sensor has a better signal is what the Pixhawk uses. If only one sensor is plugged in, it uses that sensor full time.
- **Power ports**: Contrary to what you may think, these ports are not meant to supply power to the devices that the Pixhawk controls. Rather, these ports read the status of the power source (battery) and supply voltage to the sensors and unit itself. Power to the servos, speed controllers, or other devices that the Pixhawk controls must be supplied to the servo rail via a BEC (which we'll get into when we design our first drone in `Chapter 2`, *Your First Drone - An Autonomous RC Car*.
- **MAIN OUT/AUX OUT**: These are the ports that whatever we're controlling with our Pixhawk plug into. These will usually be servos and speed controllers for motors.

Safety and best practices

This is all going to sound very obvious and like common sense. Well, it is. Unfortunately though, sometimes common sense can go right out the window when someone is excited about testing out a new vehicle. Being overly nervous can have the same effect. So, here are some basic guidelines to follow for reference:

- **Never test a new setting around people**: This is true with all types of drones. It doesn't matter if you're at a designated flying field, RC car track, or missile testing range. Choose a time when there are as few observers as possible. If things go wrong, you don't want to hurt someone.
- **Take baby steps in testing**: Did you just build a new drone? Don't go full autonomous. You never want to go full autonomous. At least not right out of the gate. First, run at full manual control to make sure all of the linkages are working properly. Then, step it up to some small autonomous maneuvers, and work your way up to flat out speed, or takeoffs and landings.
- **Leave the propellers off**: When you're making sure that power gets to the system and programming the system; remove the propellers on any air vehicles. Put any rovers up on stands to get the wheels off the ground. Elevate any boats to keep the screws off the table. If the throttle suddenly goes wide open, you don't want any personal or property damage.

- **Always remember that your drones are experimental**: The drones you build yourself are not full production machines. They don't have an entire team of engineers and quality assurance technicians, and they certainly aren't made by a corporation that can be held responsible for faulty assembly in the case of an accident. You are responsible for anything that may go wrong. Therefore, be responsible. These things can hurt or even kill people. A large 20 lb drone falling from the sky into a crowd of people is not going to make for a pleasant day for anybody.
- **Have a spotter with you**: Testing drones is a team effort. As you'll probably have your face buried in a screen monitoring telemetry data, or have target fixation on your drone trying to keep your financial investment in the air, on all four wheels, or skitting across the surface of a pond; have someone with you to advise you of obstacles and problems you may face. They can also help keep onlookers that happen by back from the danger zone. In the event of something catastrophic, they can also help you find all the pieces.

Summary

Wow, that was certainly a lot of information to take in, but at least the foundation is laid and now we can get to the fun parts! In this chapter, we learned about all the different types of drones. We also discussed some potential uses and markets for drone technology. Finally, we went over the power of the Pixhawk platform and gave you a high-level overview of how the connections plug into the Pixhawk and what each port is for. Don't worry if you're a bit confounded. It was an awful lot of information, but it will become much clearer when you see it in practice in the chapters to follow.

Now, get ready, because we're diving straight into implementing the Pixhawk into your first vehicle. In the next chapter, we'll be altering a simple RC car and using a Pixhawk to make it into an autonomous rover. A rover with an added boost, that is.

2
Your First Drone - An Autonomous RC Car

This chapter is much less about Pixhawk, and much more about how to design and alter a vehicle to implement Pixhawk. We're going to cover:

- Kitbashing
- Planning around limitations
- Planning the placement of components
- Fabricating new parts
- Basic components
- The basics of Mission Planner

Our rover

Meet the Traxxas Rustler VXL Brushless (following picture), an off-road speed demon at more than 70 mph with a 3S battery. If you're familiar with this car, you'll recognize that it is certainly not (completely) stock. Bigger, wider tires have been fitted with deeper treads for better traction and more resistance to rolling. Additionally, these tires are very soft (adding to the suspension of the vehicle) to reduce vibration on the chassis.

Finally, a wheelie bar has been added to keep it from flipping during acceleration and bumps.

You may also notice that we added a bumper to the front to protect the suspension against forward collisions. Let's get started.

Kitbashing

Kitbashing is a term coined in the cinematic miniature (the art of making miniatures for visual effects) world. It generally means buying pre-formed models (such as model airplanes made of plastic to be displayed on a shelf), taking parts from that kit, and combining it with others (or your own custom parts) to create something new. For instance, you can see parts of the original Star Wars Millenium Falcon that include guns and exhausts from various military model kits.

Some purists may think of this as cheating. They are amateurs. Professionals do it all the time. After all, where time is money, why reinvent something that already exists?

Throughout this book, we're going to use the same philosophy. We're going to take dumb objects and make them smart with the Pixhawk controller and components. On some projects, we'll even go full-kitbashing by combining two or more objects into one smart object.

Rustler VXL

Well, the philosophy and practices we're going to be using can be used on any ground vehicle with small adaptations. We're using the VXL because it's one of the cars we had lying around our shop. Plus, it's pretty darned cool, right?

But the components and practices we're using can be translated to any RC car—even the ones you may pick up at your local Wal-Mart. Going out and spending more than $400 on an RC car is certainly not required for this chapter.

Planning and limitations

"A man's got to understand his limits," said Clint Eastwood in one of the famous *Dirty Harry* movies. The same philosophy is true when designing any drone. It's always good to have more capability than is truly required. However, you certainly may consider bringing it down a notch or two in practice. You'll see what we mean in a moment.

Identifying the components

The three types of components we're going to be interfacing with on the car are the **Electronic Speed Controller** (**ESC**), receiver, and servo(s).

Most RC cars only have one servo (to steer the wheels), but sometimes multiple servos exist (for example, four-wheel steering). We'll worry about the servo later. After all, we don't need to actually get at the servo. We just need its plug (which will be attached to the receiver). Servo wires are very easily identified. They are always three wires and are either colored in a white-red-black or yellow-red-black color scheme.

The ESC is also easily identified as it is where the main power lead (plug for the battery) is attached. It regulates the power from the battery to the drive motor(s), and thus controls the speed of the motor. Should you elect to increase the power of a motor, you should keep in mind the following three things:

1. **Battery power should be weighed against the ESC**: For instance, you don't want to overpower an ESC rated for 2S or 3S batteries (2-cell or 3-cell li-po batteries) with a 4S battery. This can literally result in a fire.

2. **The type of motor**: Brushed motors (motors using brushes to change the polarity of the electromagnets within the motor) cannot use brushless ESCs. Conversely, brushless motors (motors that rely on the ESC to change the polarity of the electromagnets within the motor) cannot use brushed ESCs.

3. **The power draw of the motor**: Using a small ESC on a huge motor can (and will) result in a fire. I once put a huge motor in an RC Spitfire, and forgot to change the ESC. It came down in a ball of flames.

In the following image, you can see the ESC and the receiver box for the Rustler (after we removed the shell). You can also see the white-red-black servo control wires:

Planning the placement of Pixhawk

Immediately, we can see two possible placements for the Pixhawk once we remove the shell of the Rustler. The first image (shown next) would be an optimal place to put the Pixhawk at first glance, but is terrible upon consideration:

It's always a good idea to do a test placement of your components before mounting them. In this case, we can see that where we originally thought we could put our Pixhawk is a terrible location.

The rear of the Pixhawk overlaps the battery compartment. This means when we go to put a battery in the vehicle to drive it, it won't fit. Also, the structural support for the front suspension overlaps with several of our Pixhawk plugs. Finally, our Pixhawk would be leaning forward. If the Pixhawk is not level, it may not function properly (and absolutely would not function properly if this was an air vehicle).

You may wonder, "Why don't we just put it in sideways?" On the top of the Pixhawk, you will notice a white arrowhead on the cube. This indicates the forward direction of the Pixhawk. A deviation in placing this arrow facing forward will result in incorrect compass readings, and an inability to drive the rover properly (it may think it's pointing North, when in fact it's pointing East).

Placement number two is more optimal in some ways, but has its disadvantages too. Let's take a look at the following image:

Placing the Pixhawk on the port side (on the left side of the vehicle in this book; we will be using starboard and port references to eliminate confusion), it can remain level and unobstructed. However, as shown in the preceding image, we'll need to construct a platform for this hollowed-out area of the chassis. Let's look at it from the other side:

There is a definite overhang at the front port corner of the Pixhawk. This means that in the case of a collision or roll, the Pixhawk may sustain severe damage (especially at 70+ mph).

So, we're going to have to construct a platform for the Pixhawk that rests inside the chassis cradle and protects that front corner and the entire port side of the Pixhawk before we start connecting anything.

3D modeling, printing, and silicone molding

One of the best materials to construct a mounting platform for a Pixhawk from is Gel-10 silicone. It's the same stuff they use to make skin-like objects for masks, detached limbs for visual effects in movies, and, well, many other skin-like products. It's flexible, soft, and easily moulded. You could also make platforms from soft foam if you don't have access to these tools. We're not actually going to make this particular platform from silicone though. Why? Because the tray is too deep. The silicone would be too tall, and it would bounce around like gelatine. We're going to use a 3D-printed part. However, so that you can learn the process of mould-making, we'll make one out of silicone. The mould will be useful still, because if we crash the rover and destroy the mount, who wants to wait 3 hours for another print out? We could just use our mould and pour some two-part plastic into it. Let's give you a quick primer in making custom parts.

Measure five times, print once

Accuracy in your measurements is key. I use a calliper (rather than a simple ruler) to get the most accurate possible measurements (as shown in the following image). I also use metric (as the increments are much finer than English):

Model it in 3D

I used Lightwave 3D (an animation and modeling tool for visual effects) in the following image to create my prototype part. However, you can use Blender (free), Autocad, or any other modeling tool to create your virtual part for printing:

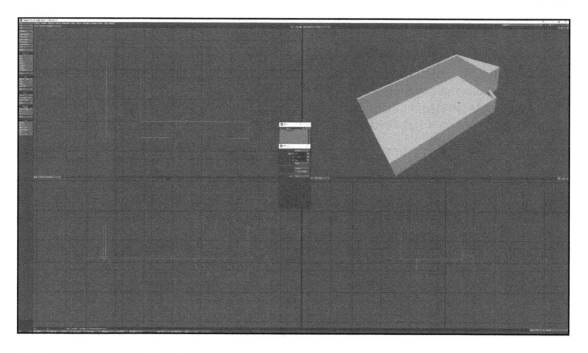

It's important to note that there are many ways to make your master for your mould. Clay modeling, wood carving, and even hot glue molding are among these methods. I prefer CAD and 3D printing as it's much more accurate, with a much more finished look.

Once it's done, it can be exported for 3D printing.

Print it in 3D

Once you've got your 3D model, you can export it in various formats (depending on your print software). 3D printing software (also called *slicing*) essentially slices the object into all the layers that a printer uses to create a 3D object in the real world. It will also help you by placing supports (shown in the following diagram) under any surfaces that may droop. These supports are then removed by you after the print has completed:

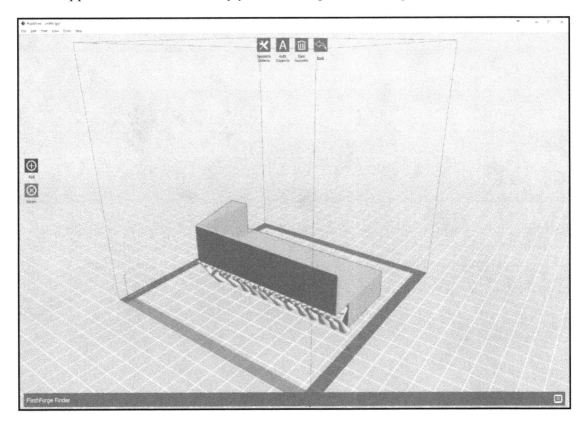

You can see the completed object in the following image. Hey, the color of filament I had loaded in my printer happened to be pink. No jokes please:

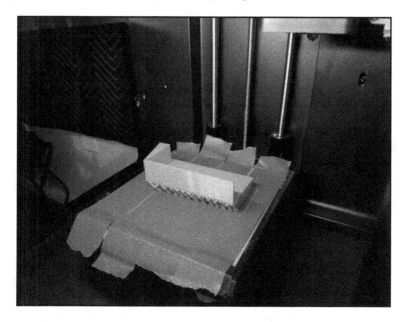

At this point, you may be wondering, "Why bother making a mould?" True, we could use this plastic **Polylactic Acid (PLA)** part for the platform as is. However, it's hard and brittle plastic. Any collisions may result in it shattering (resulting in having to re-print). So making a mould for replacement parts is highly advisable. It can easily be recast from the mould in a matter of 30 minutes (rather than the 3-hour print time). Finally, it allows you to play with different materials and try softer and harder grades of plastic, or resins, to get to just the right flexibility and dampening properties (if need be). Molding is (usually) a much better way to go than just straight 3D printing.

Before we make the mould, we need to remove the support structures and test-fit the part. There may be some **Dremmeling** (using a rotary tool to cut away and reshape the print to get it to fit just right) involved, so we want to make sure it fits perfectly before making a mould. In the following image, you can see the final fit-test (with the Pixhawk sitting in the cradle):

Preparing for molding

Since we had to Dremmel away some plastic, we end up with some holes in our part. We don't want this to affect our mould, and we'd like nice smooth parts. See, 3D prints are not solid. They are hollow with geometric shapes within them. Most commonly, they are honeycombed internally. So Dremmeling exposes these honeycombs, and they need to be filled. One quick way of filling in the holes is with hot glue. You must be careful though. Hot glue can soften your print and even melt it, so you have to work quickly and in small spurts. Burying your part in hot glue will destroy it. You can see the process of filling in the gaps of the object using hot glue in the following image:

Now, we need to make a mould container. Simple foam-core boards and some hot glue do the trick to create a box around our object, as shown in the following image. We hot-glue our part at the bottom of the mould:

Pouring the mould

Now, we mix up our silicone. For the mould itself, we're using a low-viscosity silicone that mixes at a 10-1 ratio. It's much firmer than Gel-10 and has much more resilience. It can even handle up to 500 degrees Farenheit temperatures (in case we feel like making some items out of metal). If you want a mould to last, this is just the kind of material to use.

Once the silicone is mixed, it's a good idea to put your mix into a vacuum chamber. If you don't have access to one, it's okay. But a vacuum chamber helps release any air bubbles in the silicone you just mixed. In the following image, you can see how the silicone froths up. Once a majority of the bubbles have popped, you can release the vacuum and take your silicone out. Be careful though. If your mixing containers are too full, the froth can boil over:

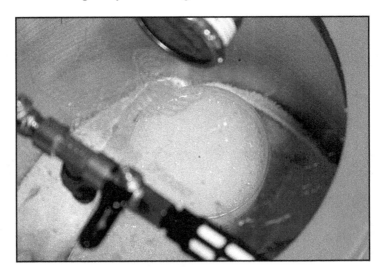

While you're waiting for the bubbles to pop, you can spray some mould-release spray into the mould box with the part inside. Be very liberal with the spray. Make sure everything is glistening. This release spray is an oily material that keeps the silicone from adhering to the box and original part. Don't wait too long though. Some silicones cure very quickly (Gel-10, for instance, completely solidifies in under 10 minutes).

Now, you can pour your silicone into the mould. Tilt the box around to different angles, and even tap on it a bit to shake any air bubbles loose. We need the silicone to get to every area of our part. Pour in enough to completely cover your part, with enough over the top to keep it from tearing when removing parts. You can see the poured mould in the following image. Notice that we added a couple of rubber bands to keep the sides from splitting during the upcoming steps:

Also notice that we left plenty of room at the top of the mould. Why? Because we're going back to the vacuum chamber to make sure we have no air bubbles around the edges of our part in the silicone. In the following image, you can see how far up the silicone froths. We don't want to make a huge mess:

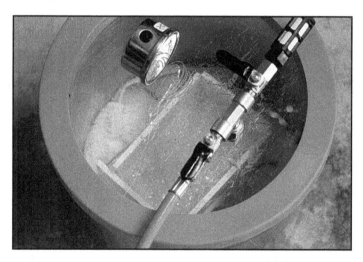

Granted, it's a bit difficult to see past the residue on the clear lid. However, if you look close, you can see that the silicone froth has come up all the way to the top of the mould box. After most of the bubbles have popped, we transfer the mould to the pressure chamber (as shown in the following image):

Again, these chambers are not required. However, it does make for better moulds. You may wonder, "Why vacuum air out, and then put it back in?" Well, we're not injecting air back into the mould. By increasing air pressure around the mould, we're forcing any remaining air bubbles within the silicone to shrink to their smallest size possible. We're also forcing silicone into all the nooks and crannies of the part. As this particular silicone sets in 30 minutes, we wait at least that long before removing the mould from the pressure tank. We increase the pressure to about 40 PSI, and let it sit.

Once the silicone is set (we test by checking the leftovers in our mixing containers), we remove it from the pressure tank, and begin the demolding and curing process.

Demolding and curing

When taking a part out of a mould, you have to be very firm but extremely patient. You don't want to pull so hard on a part that you break it (or tear the mould), and you don't want to work so soft that nothing gets done. Once the master part is removed, you have a little factory for creating more parts. Just mix some plastic, spray some mould release, and put it in your chambers the same way as before.

The final step before you store the mould is making sure it lasts. Silicone cures under UV light (most silicones at least). You can always buy some UV lights and make your own curing chamber. Mine is a simple ice chest with a white liner, and a string of LED UV lights. Letting it sit in the box overnight should be good enough (as shown in the following image):

So, why did we spend so much time on mould making? Because being able to make your own parts is crucial in drone design. These are electronic and mechanical beasts. You must be able to mount your sensors securely, and you may even need to make custom parts for other purposes (as we'll see in Chapter 3, *A Drone for Hunters - Autonomous Duck Decoy)*. Why not get it out of the way as soon as possible?

Hooking up your Pixhawk

Now that we have somewhere to put our Pixhawk, we can go over how to attach it and program it for a basic rover. The Pixhawk comes with several strips of ¼"—thick foam tape. This stuff is great. It absorbs vibrations and shocks to the Pixhawk that could potentially throw off sensor readings. Before using it though, make sure you clean off your part. Mould-release spray is very oily stuff, and is meant to keep things from sticking together. Simple liquid dishwashing soap does the trick perfectly. I like Dawn, as it cuts grease especially well and is easy to rinse off.

We can just hot glue our mount into the frame of the rover, and then foam tape the Pixhawk in. Notice that the USB port is still above the side guard to allow access for programming, as shown in the following image:

Our Pixhawk is level, secure, protected, and pink. The first component we're going to hook up will be the GPS.

Global Positioning System (GPS)

Although we can hook up two GPS antennas for more accuracy, as the process is the same for both, we're only going to use one. Besides, we're a bit pressed for space on this rover.

The first thing you'll notice is with most GPS antennas, the plugs do not match. In fact, they don't on most components you'll buy for Pixhawk 2.1. The powers that be have elected to change the plug configuration to something of an entirely different shape. Although these plugs are far superior to previous versions (they lock in place and can obviously only fit in one way); it means that changing plug ends is needed.

Luckily, the Pixhawk 2.1 comes with patch-style plugs (male at both ends). One end plugs into the new plugs, while the other goes to the older version. We need to remove each wire from the plugs (on both the older version end, and on the end from our component) one at a time and solder them together. Matching the wires is a matter of placing them end to end, with one plug upside down and the other right side up, as shown in the following image:

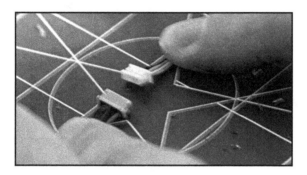

You can't rely on the color of the wires. Notice that the one on the right is rainbow colored, while the one on the left is all black with one red wire. You must have one plug flipped to match them up. Notice how the lighter plug (top-right) has little silver dots along the top (actually indents exposing the pins), while the darker plug (lower left) is completely flat on top. This is how to match them up to make sure you attach the wires properly. Doing it wrong can damage your component and/or the Pixhawk.

Removing the wires from the plug is a simple matter of using something sharp to push down on that indent (which exposes the pin), and gently pulling the wire out of the plug as shown in the following image:

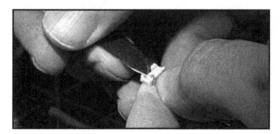

As each pin is removed from each side, solder them together one at a time. Doing all of them at once can and will lead to confusion.

Wrap each solder with either heat-shrink or electrical tape, and then wrap the whole bundle with more tape (as shown in the following image):

Now, where shall we place the GPS? Much like the main Pixhawk, GPS modules usually contain a compass. Thus, you should look for the arrow on top. This should always point forward, regardless of where the cable is attached. We decided to put our GPS up front (where we were originally thinking the Pixhawk could go). This keeps it well away from the electromagnetic interference that a motor can produce. It should be easy to keep it clear up here on the nose of the vehicle (as shown in the following image):

You can also see that the GPS antenna is now plugged into the GPS1 port. Using 3M automotive body tape to secure components is a great way to do it. It's very strong tape, double sided, and flexible. You can pick it up at any autoparts store.

The GPS 1 cable (which comes with the Pixhawk) also has an arm button. This button allows you to get everything going without activating any motors or servos. Once you're ready to roll, you just hold down this button for a couple of seconds. We'll get to that in just a bit.

Radio telemetry

Cool word, right? We hear it said by space agencies when talking about spacecraft that "telemetry is showing all is nominal." Nominal another great word. Telemetry is just data, data from a remote source sent to another point. In this case, telemetry would be all the sensor data from your rover (for example, GPS) to your computer via a wireless link. Conversely, data can be sent back. This is how we control the autonomous functions of the rover. You can think of it as basically a wireless USB cable that has a range of great distances (depending on the terrain and interference of course). The telemetry module we're using can actually have a range in terms of miles.

You'll need to use the same methods to join the telemetry module to our cable for the Telem 1 plug as we did with GPS. The main thing to keep in mind with the radio telemetry module is to keep it well away from the GPS and control receiver. There just happens to be a nice, large, flat spot on the front of the Pixhawk mount we made (as shown in the following image):

RC receiver

Although we could just control the whole thing with our computer (using the telemetry module and a joystick), we prefer a traditional tactile controller. Plus, it's always a good idea to have more than one method of control.

Pixhawk works with several different types of controller standards (Futaba, Spektrum/JR, even a simple receiver with individual outputs for every channel of control). We're going to use the Spektrum standard.

There is a plug just for Spektrum (satellite receivers) on the top of the Pixhawk. There are also plugs for Futaba standards. It works pretty much the same. Luckily, the Spektrum and Futaba controllers have a standardized plug, so no soldering is necessary. Just plug the receiver into the SPKT port and place the receiver. We put ours on the very front of the rover (just in front of the GPS antenna) as shown in the following image:

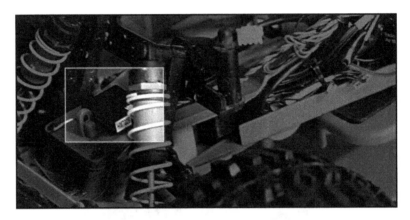

Connecting the brain to the body

Now, we need to hook up the Pixhawk to the power, the motor, and the steering. If we open the receiver box, we'll see three servo (white, red, and black) cables. One goes to the ESC to control the motor. The other goes to the steering servo. There are a plethora of servo connections on the rear of the Pixhawk, as shown in the following image:

The steering servo (the servo wire leading to the front of the vehicle) connects to **Main Out pin 1** vertically, with the wire at the top being black (ground) and the white wire going to the bottom. The throttle servo wire connects to **Main Out pin 3** in the same way.

Finally, connect the power lead to power 1 (as also shown in the following image), and connect the other end to the power module (as shown in the following image):

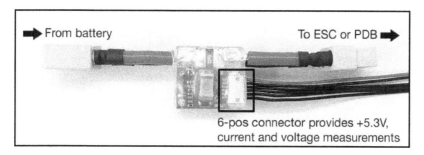

This power module goes inline (between the battery and speed controller) to provide power to the Pixhawk's computer and give power readings (so the Pixhawk knows when it's running low on power).

This does not provide power to the servos. The servo board must get power from a **Battery Eliminator Circuit** (**BEC**), a device that eliminates the need for multiple batteries by distributing power to the servo board. The ESC on this rover has a BEC integrated into it. So, it not only receives signals from the Pixhawk, but supplies power to all the servos. If this ESC didn't have a BEC integrated, one would be needed (connected directly to the main battery), and could be plugged into any port on the servo board (rear of the Pixhawk). Most ESCs have BECs integrated. However, some do not, and it's important to know what a BEC is.

Now that everything is hooked up, let's get started with the software.

Programming the Pixhawk for our (basic) rover

There are two pieces of (free) software that you'll want. The first is your primary Pixhawk software (Mission Planner). The other is QgroundControl. Both are available from multiple sources, and a simple Google search will get you both.

Although we have the radio telemetry unit installed, on our very first startup of Pixhawk we're going to need to directly connect it to a computer via USB. Remember that plug on the side of the Pixhawk cube? That's our computer USB plug. It's best to use a laptop (so you can use it in the field).

The wizard

After connecting the Pixhawk to our computer, start up the Mission Planner software. You'll be confronted with this requestor:

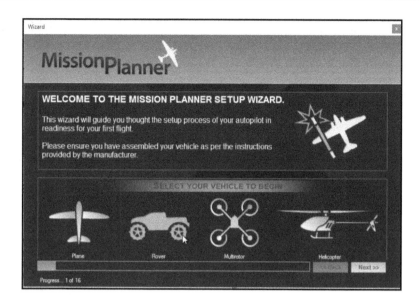

Obviously, you'll want to select **Rover**. This wizard will do the initial setup of your Pixhawk and calibrate it for use.

Next you simply select how the computer connects to the Pixhawk (as shown in the following screenshot):

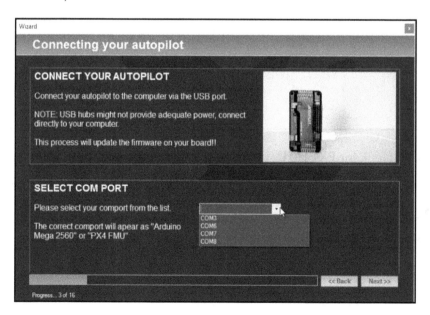

At this point, you must provide which port the Pixhawk is attached to. The Pixhawk essentially emulates a serial port via USB (a COM port). The way to know which port is associated with your Pixhawk (on Windows) is to look at the **Device Manager** (as shown in the following screenshot):

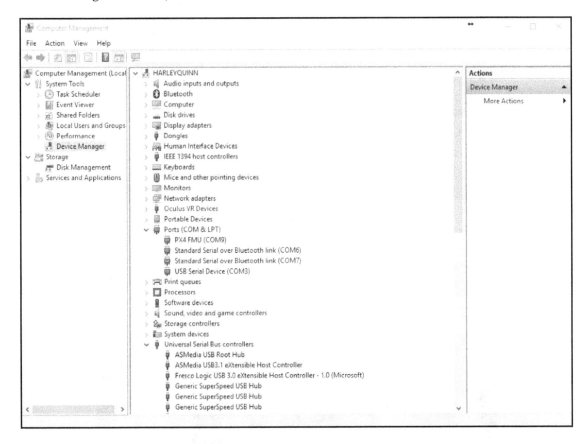

Under **Ports**, just look for **PX4 FMU**. In this case, you can see that it's **COM9**.

Now that it's found the Pixhawk, it will verify its version of firmware and update it. If this fails, just repeat the steps until it succeeds. You may need to change which plug you have the USB jacked into. Sometimes USB hubs and other devices can interfere. Again, just keep trying with different combinations until it works. It will eventually. In most cases, it works the first time.

The next step is compass calibration. Wherever the device is in the world, the compass needs to be calibrated. Additionally, every time the drone is used, you should recalibrate the compass. Solar flares, electric lines, and buildings can create variances in the Earth's magnetic field at your location. It's extremely important to have an accurate compass reading.

For this stage, you'll see this screen:

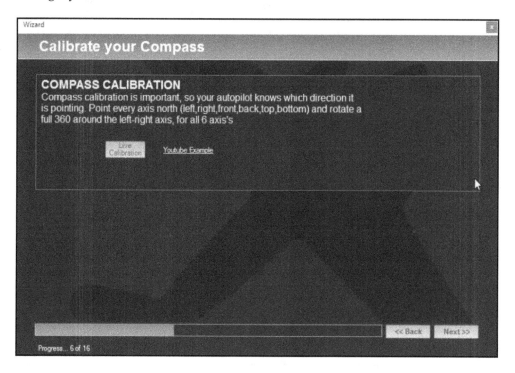

While this is onscreen (with the cable still connected), take the rover and spin it on all 6 axes a full 360 degrees. This lets the rover sense the magnetic field in all directions and know which way it is facing.

Next, the wizard will move into configuring the power monitor module (as shown in the following screenshot):

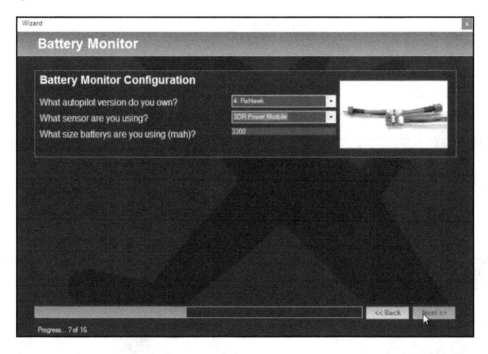

We need to make sure the communication protocols are accurate with the device. If you're not sure which power module you have, a safe bet is to select the **3DR Power Module** option.

As for the size of batteries, this is in reference to the mAh (milliamp hours) rating. 1000 mAh means that for one hour, it can supply a constant current of 1 Amp (1000 milliamps). The mAh rating is stamped on all batteries. If it is in Amp-hours (Ah) instead of milliamp hours (mAh), just multiply the number by 1000 to fill in this field.

After clicking on **Next**, the wizard will have you set up any sonar devices (as shown in the following screenshot):

We're not using sonar for this rover. However, we may use it in a much later chapter. So we just left the **Sonar Model** field at **None**.

On to the control configuration. Here is where we can bind the receiver to our control transmitter (a Spektrum DX8 in this case) and calibrate the controls to work properly.

The following screenshot shows the screens associated with this process:

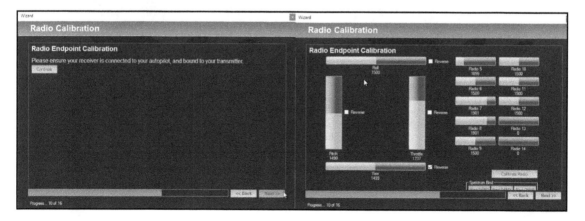

In the panel on the left, you'll see a **Continue** button (not the **Next** button). That will bring you to the panel on the right. At the lower-right, you'll notice a section called **Spektrum Bind**. Activating the proper binding button by selecting the appropriate type of **Spektrum Satellite** will set the receiver into bind mode. Then, just follow the instructions in the Spektrum manual for binding whichever Spektrum transmitter you are using. For the DX8, the following are the instructions:

1. Select a fresh model
2. Turn the transmitter off
3. Hold down the **Bind** button
4. Turn on the transmitter while holding the **Bind** button
5. Wait for the transmitter to confirm it is bound

After binding the transmitter, just click on the **Calibrate Radio** button and follow the instructions. (It will have you move various controls in different directions.)

Next is the **Flight Modes** setting, as shown in the following screenshot:

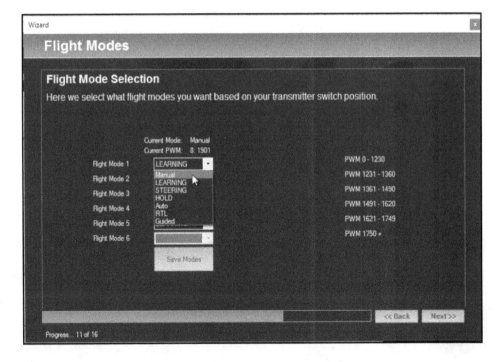

Up to seven flight modes can be associated with a switch or dial on your remote. If you have a three-position switch on the remote, modes 1, 3, and 5 are the most likely ones that would be assigned to these positions. The flight modes are as follows:

- **Manual**: This mode involves full manual control of the vehicle. The Pixhawk simply forwards all commands directly to the servos and ESCs it is controlling.
- **LEARNING**: This mode has the same controls as the manual mode, but it lets you toggle a switch on your controller to teach GPS waypoints to the software for use in the **Auto** mode. Essentially, the rover will repeat your movements.
- **STEERING**: This mode is the same as the Learning mode, but turns on obstacle avoidance (if sonar is used), and will steer the rover around obstacles for you. This is great for tuning your obstacle avoidance (which we may use in a later chapter).
- **HOLD**: This mode stops the rover with all wheels stopped and pointed straight ahead.
- **Auto**: This mode involves fully autonomous driving from waypoint to waypoint. This waypoint list will be looped and repeated infinitely. If reception is lost, the rover will go in to the **HOLD** mode.
- **RTL**: This stands for **Return to Launch** and will directly return the rover to the spot it was launched from. Upon reaching the launch point, it will go into the **HOLD** mode. If sonar-equipped, it will avoid obstacles along the way.
- **Guided**: This mode utilizes the radio telemetry unit. You can use advanced controls (such as telling the throttle to let up if the rover pulls a wheelie), use joysticks on the computer, or specify waypoints on the fly. Think of this as the **Mars Rover** setting.

On the final screen of the wizard, you should see that everything is green except for trying to arm your rover (as shown in the following screenshot):

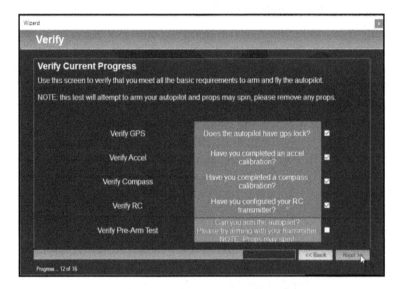

Do not try to arm your rover at this point. First, perform the following procedure:

1. Make sure all four wheels are off the ground. We used an RC car stand (the orange platform in all of the pictures of the rover in this chapter).
2. Make sure your transmitter is on.
3. Connect the power sensor module to the ESC.
4. Connect the battery to the power sensor module.
5. Hold down the ARM button (the now flashing red button attached to the GPS cable) for 3 seconds.

If the red button light stops flashing and goes solid red... congratulations. It has successfully armed. If not, or if the button's light never turned on, you may have connected up the wrong wires on the GPS cabling. Check them again.

The red box will not turn green, but you have registered successful arming in every significant way.

The rest of the screens do not actually allow you to configure anything. They simply advise you of what **Failsafe** options are and give you some links for some reading material. Read them. They are very helpful.

More calibration...

No matter how cool everything looks right now, stop! You may be seeing a map and some cool readouts. First, we need to calibrate the accelerometers. Click on the **INITIAL SETUP** tab at the top of the Mission Planner software, and you'll get to the following screen:

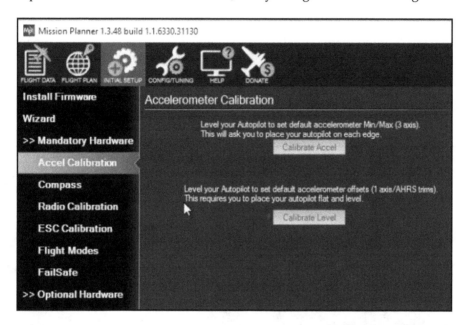

Along the left of the screen is **Accel Calibration** (under the **Mandatory Hardware** tab). Click on each of the buttons (**Calibrate Accel** and **Calibrate Level**) in the interface and follow the onscreen instructions. This calibrates the accelerometers so that the Pixhawk knows exactly what the attitude of the craft is. You will be required to put the rover in several positions and put it level. We advise you to do this under USB power without the battery connected.

You may need to also calibrate the ESC for your drive wheels. Again, just follow the simple onscreen instructions for this step.

Testing and driving

Before we take it out to the field, we'll want to test the connections. Close the Mission Planner software, remove the USB cable, and attach the USB telemetry dongle to your computer. With the wheels off the ground, power on your transmitter and rover by plugging the battery in, but do not arm the rover.

After starting the Mission Planner software, you may be asked again to find the rover's com port. In your device manager, the telemetry unit should be visible under the Ports tab, this time as a Silicon Labs device.

Upon successfully finding the telemetry dongle, you'll see this screen inside Mission Planner:

After clicking on the **Connect** button (top right of the interface), you should see your rover at your location. Yep... that's my house.

Let's do some initial tuning and show you how it's done. Before we actually drive the rover, we need to make sure it's not just going to speed away at 70+ mph into oblivion.

At this point, with the telemetry module communicating with the computer, we can do anything we could do with USB. If you go to the `Config Tuning` tab at the top, it lets us set up some limits for the speed of our rover (as shown in the following screenshot):

Inside the **Standard Params** tab on the left, you'll find **Target Cruise Speed** and **Base Throttle Percentage** (as we saw earlier). We set our cruise speed at 5 meters per second and our throttle percentage at 15%. This way, on autopilot the throttle doesn't go above 15% and the speed doesn't exceed 5 meters per second-nice and slow.

Drive the rover around a lot before ever attempting an autopilot. We'll get deeper into tuning later. But for a rover, these two speed settings are essential. We can gradually increase them later if we wish.

Setting waypoints

We're going to get much deeper into this in the next chapter. However, setting waypoints is as simple as clicking on the map on the main screen of Mission Planner. The only thing we really want to say at this point is that it risks everything. Your drone may crash, and could even hurt someone. We don't intend this chapter to show you how to create a waypoint drone. This one does not even have collision avoidance. However, this chapter was to familiarize you with the methodology of creating a rover-style drone, and the basic connections and configuration of Pixhawk 2.1.

This drone is waypoint capable though. If you must try it out, do it in a completely empty area where no people or property will get hurt.

For a full explanation of waypoints and autonomous driving, refer to the next chapter.

Summary

In this chapter, we learned how to fabricate parts and connect up the older peripherals to the brand new Pixhawk 2.1. We got into the configuration wizard, and even touched on the telemetry module.

In the next chapter, we'll get deeper into all of these things with our first purpose-built drone, a duck decoy. This decoy will autonomously troll around a pond and attract ducks for hunters. We'll use everything we learned here and get into waypoints and patrolling with rovers.

So, buckle up... here we go!

3
A Drone for Hunters – Autonomous Duck Decoy

A water rover is really no different than setting up a land rover drone; with one serious exception—water + electronics = bad... really bad. So, special attention needs to be paid to the waterproofing of your drone. In this regard, some special techniques, materials, and mechanics need to be employed to keep water out, keep your drone upright, and keep it alive while floating in an environment that completely destroys electronics.

In this chapter, we'll be wrapping up some of our manufacturing techniques, as well as getting a bit more into Pixhawk. But mostly, we'll show you how similar a boat is to a rover. We'll be covering:

- Coming up with ideas for drones
- Making your ideas marketable
- More on manufacturing and fabrication
- Foresight of design challenges
- The design workflow
- Waterproofing

Let's start with, "Why a duck decoy?" After all, doesn't that seem like a waste of Pixhawk? Isn't Pixhawk used for huge prototype medical drones? Isn't Pixhawk something meant for gazillion-dollar (to make and sell) ideas?

Spawning a marketable deal

As any business major can tell you, the key to making money on a product is the law of supply and demand. The key here is demand. The best ideas●the ideas that changed the world and made the inventor a ton of capital—aren't necessarily the ideas that cater to a customer with an uber-budget. The wheel, the mouse trap, even the scrub-daddy are multimillion (even billion) dollar ideas that everyone can use, most can afford, and solve a basic problem.

Personally, I don't hunt, full disclosure. I've never been duck hunting. However, I have noticed that those I do know (who hunt) have duck decoys—lots of them. Different decoys for different types of ducks, and often they come back with fewer decoys than they left with.

Also, hunting is boring. Go out to an area and wait, and wait, and keep waiting until eventually some ducks show up. What if you could make the waiting process more fun? What if you could drive a duck around on the pond, or even let it drive itself and navigate the pond? What if you could show off a new toy to your buddies that they don't have? And most importantly, what if (when you're done for the day) you could have your duck return to you?

It solves some problems, it has the show-off factor, and it also caters to an industry that is spread throughout the country where accessories are essential and people spend a boatload (pun intended) on these accessories.

Best of all, even though you'd be using existing technology, the idea is potentially patentable! There are tons of ideas that use existing tech in new ways that have patents. So, not only can you make an item that is marketable... it's an idea that you could license and sit back and let money roll in. These are all great reasons to make a duck decoy drone.

As I said, I'm not a hunter. I love aircraft (especially the F-117 stealth fighter). So, knowing nothing about ducks (really), nor the hunting thereof, I made my duck decoy with a faceted design just to make the prototyping phase more fun. So meet the stealth duck (also known as Black Ops McDuck), as shown in the following image:

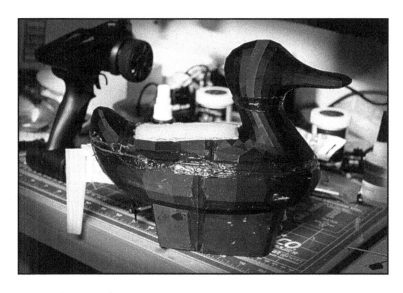

As you can see, it's 3D printed. But at least it's not pink, right?

Outlining the scope before you design

Before we actually start putting pencil to paper (or rather mouse to CAD, in this case), we need to outline some basic needs and layout of the duck. Let's start with the problems and solutions analysis that we did on the design.

The following table lists the problems and solutions we worked up; although the original table was handwritten, this one is far more legible:

Problems we'll encounter	Solutions
Water leaking into seams of the model	CA glue seams, and fill with silicone sealant.
Water leaking into the location where the propeller shaft meets up with the body	Stationary sleeve for shaft filled with grease and sealed (on the outside) with silicone.
Water leak on access lid	Silicone sealant o-ring.
In event of water leak, waterproofing Pixhawk	Silicone moulded Pixhawk case? (No).

Pixhawk heat from silicone moulded case?	Can't seal it. Must make body as water-tight as possible. Test water-tightness in every stage leading up to Pixhawk integration.
GPS reception with internal antennae	Shouldn't be a problem with a PLA plastic body.
Motor EM interference with GPS	Place motor up front and GPS antennae toward the back.
Motor heat in a sealed body	Water cooled motor.
ESC heat in a sealed body	Water cooled ESC, or low-voltage ESC / Motor.
Expense of motor, drive shaft, and prop	Kitbash a cheap RC boat.
Balancing motor, ESC, and prop for efficiency	Kitbash a cheap RC boat.
Duck is too large for 3D printer	Print in sections, use CA glue to join, and seal with silicone when dry.
Interfacing Pixhawk with cheap RC boat parts	Make sure the boat we buy is modular (not integrated ESC or servo into receiver) or at least minimize integrated parts so we have to replace as few parts as possible.
What if we want the head to turn with rudder?	Don't do this on initial prototype. But print head as a separate section so it can be adapted later if we want.
PLA plastic print or ABS?	PLA for the body (cheaper). But ABS for motor mount (higher melting temperature).
Tipping from waves or turns?	Large ballast section filled with modeling clay.

We had other problems that we encountered along the way, which were unforeseen. We'll get to these later. But as you can see from the details in our overview chart, we tried to minimize these as much as possible. Positive thinking is great. But when planning, you have to be your own nay-sayer in order to predict the problems you'll have. Then, you can think positively to come up with solutions.

You can also see that we had to compromise on the possibility of a leak destroying our Pixhawk. We wanted to create a silicone case for it in order to seal it. We thought of creating silicone dummy-plugs. We even thought of sealing the edges around the cube section. In the end though, we came to the conclusion that doing this on a possibility was outweighed by the certainty of frying our Pixhawk from heat. The cube section is actually heated (by design) to allow Pixhawk to operate in cold weather. Electronics don't like heat. And too much heat can even melt soldered components and cause shorts. So we decided to focus our waterproofing efforts on making very sure that no water can get in before integrating the Pixhawk.

Next, we sketched up a basic design for BlackOps McDuck (as shown in the following figure):

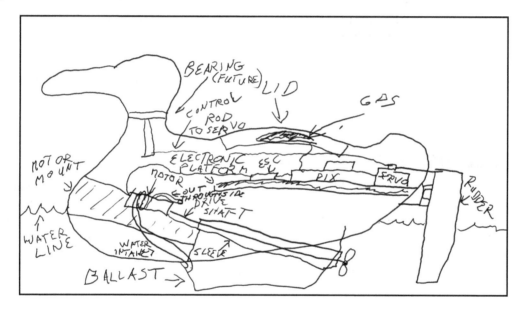

Hard to tell what's what, right? The sketch isn't a plan. It's more like a process of just working out how things will go, so that you can see problems as you're thinking about it. A sketch is very quick (5-15 minutes), and lets you think about things. Here, you can see that we moved our electronics above the water-line (in case of minor leaks). We also worked out where water would come in (in the ballast section, front), and be ejected (through the side) of our motor's water cooling. In other words, we now know that we need to carve a channel into our clay ballast so that the water intake, and the drive shaft can be well below the water line. We also discovered that the rudder needs to be quite tall.

Why would the rudder need to be tall? To accommodate the fact that our servo is well above the water line. Also, you don't want the rudder just in the water. You want it to be in the path of the propeller's thrust (so that at low speed it can vector the water being pushed and allow for more agility).

Also, we planned out how the head would turn (on a future version) using a sleeve and bearing with a shaft going down to a control rod. This rod would extend to the rear of the craft and connect to the same servo driving the rudder (allowing the head to turn and face the direction the duck turns).

Is the sketch hard to read? Yes, for everyone except the person drawing it. That's normal. That's also why it's important for the person who will make the design to be in on the sketch session (or even to draw the sketch). That's an important thing to know for larger teams. Never do a sketch without the designer around. The designer not only needs to know where everything goes, but needs to know why. This allows them to adapt the design to overcome problems they may find with the sketch (while staying true to the spirit of it).

Next, we need to order our kitbash boat. We'll need to know the basic dimensions of our hardware before designing the duck. After all everything needs to fit, right?

Choosing the kitbash boat

We are mostly looking for something cheap with a water-cooled motor. If we order from Amazon, it's pretty rare that you can take a look inside to see if things are modular (not an integrated **electronic speed control** (**ESC**) or servo). We have plenty of ESCs and servos in our workshop so we didn't care much. But if you don't have a ton of spare parts lying around, you may consider making the trip to a local hobby shop to look at the inner workings of a boat before you buy. Here's the boat we picked up (as shown in the following image):

UDI RC

Udirc Venom 2.4GHz High Speed Remote Control Electric Boat (Orange)

⭐⭐⭐⭐✰ ▾   471 customer reviews | 122 answered questions

Price: $39.99 **FREE Shipping** for Prime members Details ▾

Buy 1, get a discount on selected products   4 Applicable Promotion(s) ▾

Only 4 left in stock - order soon.
Sold by WindyFashion and Fulfilled by Amazon. Gift-wrap available.

- This newest USB-rechargeable electric RC speedboat from UDIRC will blow the others out of the water when it races by at 25 km/h (15 mph).
- It features a rugged ABS anti-tilt hull, and a water-cooled, single-prop powerful 370-size motor that combines style, speed, and affordability.
- Low battery alarm warns you when the boat is almost out of power so you know when to head for the shore. Self-righting feature lets you keep your boat in play even if it capsizes.
- The UDI001 is an exciting speedboat to see in action and even more exciting to pilot.
- When water gets into the boat, the motors, battery and servo are wet and can easily cause a short circuit if the operator doesn't make the boat dry enough. In this case, we suggest customers to dry the boat enough and make sure there is no wires or anything else twining around the motor before charging and operating again, especially the motor and the battery plug.

Roll over image to zoom in

It moves at up to 15 mph (far faster than our duck will swim), but this means that it'll have plenty of power to move our (much heavier) duck at a speed of around 3-4 mph. It may even reach 10 mph. We'll never drive it at that speed, but we like to follow Clarence's rule—it's better to have something and not need it, than to need it and not have it. This rule got its name from the movie *True Romance*. In it, the character "Clarence" says, "it's better to have a gun and not need it than to need a gun and not have it." Clarence's rule is just replacing the word "gun" with anything else.

It also has a battery and remote. So, if we wish, we can test-drive the duck before implementing the Pixhawk. We won't do this, but it's nice to have this ability if you want it.

Once the boat arrived, we carefully removed all the parts. It meant cutting the hull (so don't bother buying a warranty) to get some out. But we were careful not to destroy any wires or water tubing.

The following image shows the boat with the lid-off and all the electronics still installed:

And the following image shows all of the parts removed from the boat:

With all the parts laid out, you can see the sleeve that the drive shaft runs through (foreground with a white clump of silicone on it), and the drive shaft (right side of image next to the black propeller)

Now, we can measure all our parts (especially the motor), and design the duck body.

Designing the duck body for 3D printing

Even if you don't own a 3D printer, designing for one is handy. Plus, you can always ship your designs off to a friend, or service that does have such a device. You should eventually get one though, and they are relatively inexpensive nowadays.

One of the beauties of **Computer Aided Design** (**CAD**) is that you don't actually have to use CAD software to create objects in the real world. Confused? Don't be. CAD design and 3D animation software use very similar methodologies for modeling objects. They even share (some) file formats. And any 3D modeling software (worth its salt) can import and export in CAD formats.

You don't have to spend a boatload on AutoCAD or SolidWorks to create and prototype your designs. These programs can cost thousands of dollars (per year, or even per month) to own. Instead, you can use free software such as Blender to model your objects. The additional benefit to these easily accessed software packages is that there are tons of YouTube videos and tutorials on their use around the internet.

I'm a 3D animator by education. I've used just about every software package to create this. For modeling, I like Lightwave 3D only because it's what I learned on originally (back in 1995). If this was for a feature film, I'd probably use something else. But the methodologies (regardless of software package) I show here are universal in any modeling package (from Blender to Maya, and even in AutoCAD to SolidWorks).

The basics of 3D modeling

Before we start, here's what we want to end up with for the outer-hull of our duck:

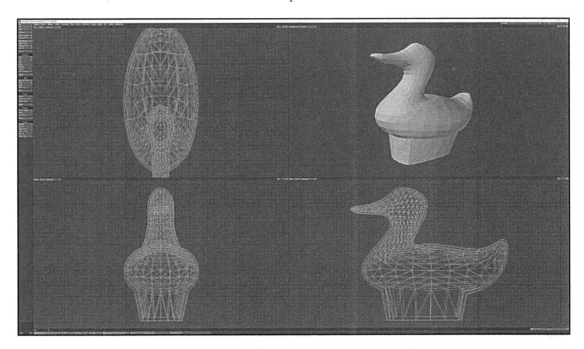

It may be hard to see, but you'll notice that the duck isn't solid. Instead, there is an inner duck and outer duck. The easiest way to see this is to look along the outline on the lower-left of the preceding diagram. This means the duck will be hollow, and you can see that the bottom-hull of the ballast section is thicker than the rest of the duck. This is because it needs to hold the weight of the clay, and be stronger in the event that our duck runs aground.

You'll also notice that the duck (although in the upper-right it appears to be made up of 4-sided polygons), is made up of triangles. Remember geometry? three points define a plane. So, 3D printers like triangle polygons (rather than quads).

Here's something you need to know before we show you how it was modeled. There are (essentially) two types of models—the ones based on polygons (where each set of points is joined by straight lines) and the ones based on curves (where they come out much smoother). 3D printers *don't work with curves*. You must use polygons.

Curves are much easier to work with (as they use fewer points to define the geometry... as you'll see). So, what we're going to do is start with curves, and convert it to polygons. This is called working with *subdivs* (or subdivided polygons).

Thoroughly confused? Good, let's clear it up for you.

Modeling with subdivs

Exactly why would you work with a subdivided polygon model, and what is it? The easiest way is to show it to you. The following image shows three versions of the same object:

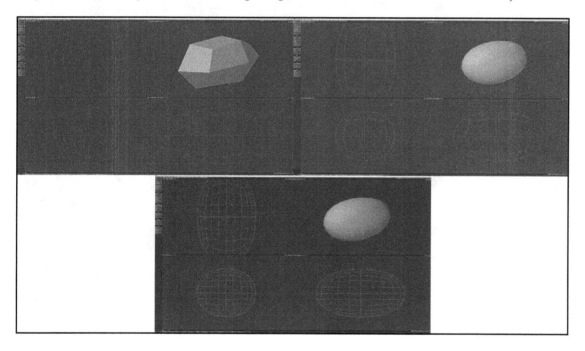

It may be difficult to see, but the screen on the upper-left shows our base object—a pure-polygonal object. It's very faceted, and doesn't even resemble an egg-shape. Converting the object to a subdiv (or curve-based object), it smooths out and becomes round (upper-right). Converting the curves back to polygons (bottom) it creates a lot more polygons. So, when modeling, it's easier to work with fewer polygons, but you get the advantage of working with curves and more detail. You get to have your cake and eat it too.

Now, exactly how does a newbie to 3D modeling get up and running quickly? Box modeling.

Box modeling 101

There are many different methods for creating 3D models. But box modeling is one of the easiest. Other methods can produce greater detail, and can be much better for animating. But box modeling can let you create an object quickly, and with minimal pain and boredom. So what is it?

It's one of the closest techniques to modeling with clay that you can use. It's called box modeling because that's what you start with, a box (as shown in the following diagram):

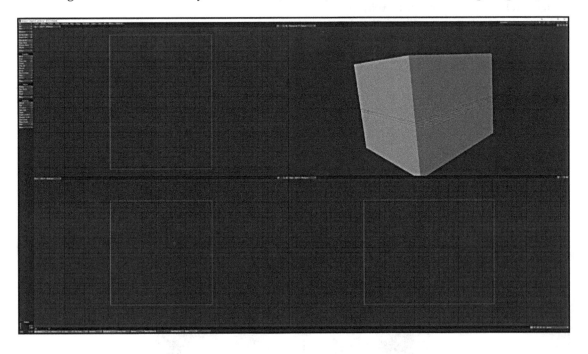

Then, we convert the object into subdiv polygons (in lightwave 3D, you just hit the *Tab* key), as shown in the following diagram:

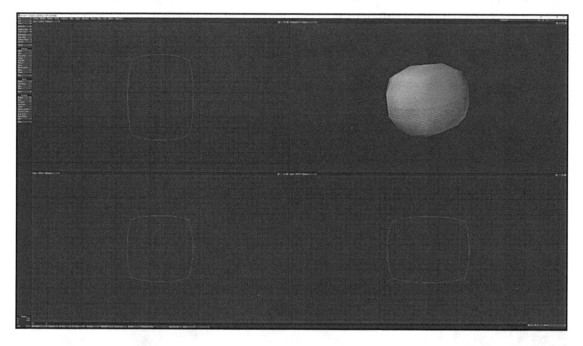

So, it turns into more of a ball shape. And there you have it you're now working with subdivs. Now, let's talk about the tools.

Knifing polygons

Sometimes you need more polygons just so you can create more detail. There are different ways of doing this to create polygons that fit different needs. The first way is to knife them. This just means that you're cutting through the polygons in a straight line to create more points that you can play with. In the following diagram, we knifed the object on each axis, and dragged the center points in each view to make our object into more of a ball. You may recognize this object from an earlier diagram:

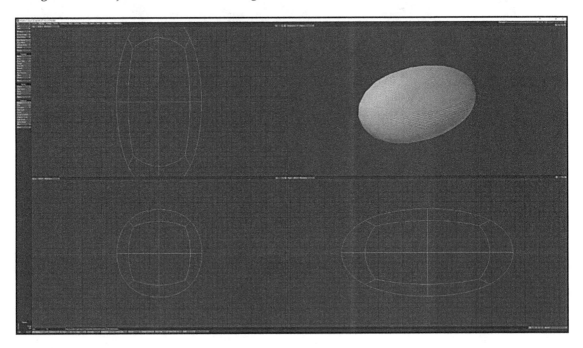

Extruding and shifting

Another way of creating more detail is to extrude and shift polygons. Essentially, you're grabbing a chunk of the digital clay, magically adding more mass to it, and pulling it off in a direction to create more detail.

To do this, you select polygons, and extrude them off the side of the object. You can then resize the polygon, rotate it, drag its points around, and so on to create your shape. The following diagram shows the side-view of the steps we used to create the head of our duck:

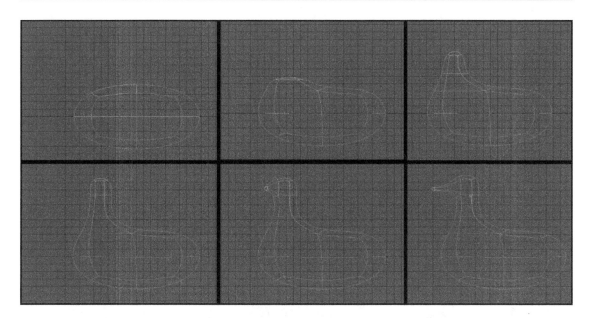

Let's take a closer look at how all this worked:

- **Top-left**: The polygons were selected on the top-front of the object
- **Top-middle**: The polygons were extruded, shifted up, and resized to form the base of the neck
- **Top-right**: The process was repeated to form the base of the head
- **Bottom-left**: The process was extruded and shifted again to form the top of the head
- **Bottom-middle**: The front of the head was selected, extruded, and resized to form the base of the duck bill
- **Bottom-right**: The process was extruded once more to form the end of the bill

As you can see, this is much easier to do than most people think. A little bit of dragging some points around and you'll end up with a good-looking head. This process is repeated for the ballast area, and a knife is used along with some point-dragging so that we can form the tail of the duck. The end result looks like this:

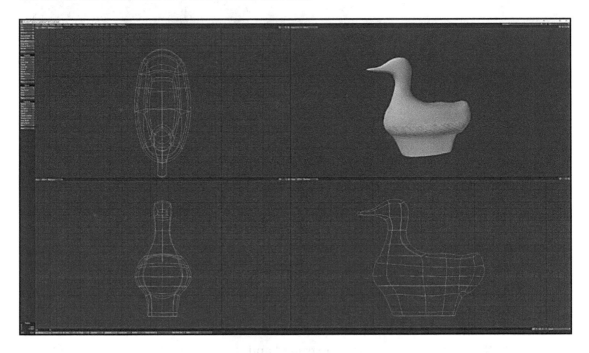

Making the duck hollow

Before converting the curves to polygons (subdividing), let's just switch back to straight polygons for a moment to make the duck hollow. You'll notice (in the following diagram) that the duck looks pretty ugly. Don't worry about it, we'll go back to curves soon:

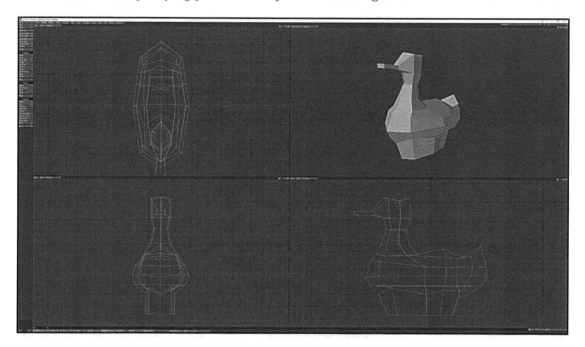

There are a few ways we could make the duck hollow. One is with Booleans (which we'll cover later). We're simply going to use a method called thicken. This thickens each polygon. In the event of a closed object (a solid), it makes the object hollow. Thickening allows us to control just how thick the walls of our hollow object are. In this case, we made the object 1/8" thick (as shown in the following diagram), and then went back to curved mode:

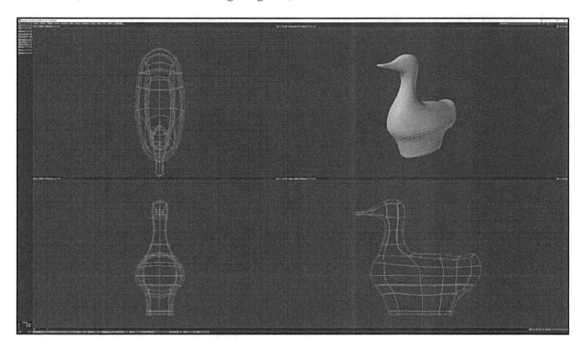

Now, we'll make our object polygonal.

Freezing curves into polygons – subdividing

Creating polygons is really easy from subdivs. Every software package works slightly differently. In Lightwave, we simply use the `freeze` command (*Ctrl + D*). But as you can see (in the following diagram), our polygons are still not triangles. They're still quads:

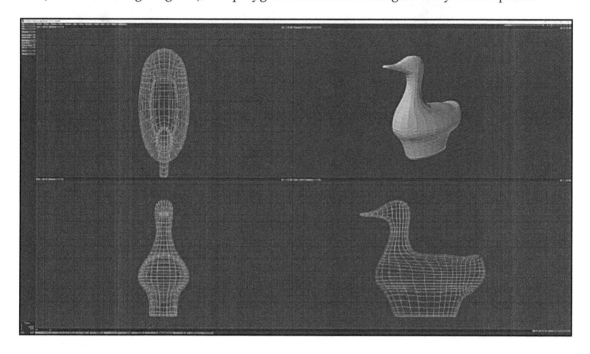

Before we get into making triangles, you'll notice that the duck is still highly faceted. It's easy enough to fix. You could just make this into curves again, and re-freeze it. This will greatly multiply the number of polygons. Every time you perform this process, your object will keep getting smoother. Our duck is stealth, so we'll leave it this way.

Again, every software package has a way of converting four-sided polygons (quads) into three-sided polygons (triangles). In Lightwave, it's just the triple command. It'll look like this:

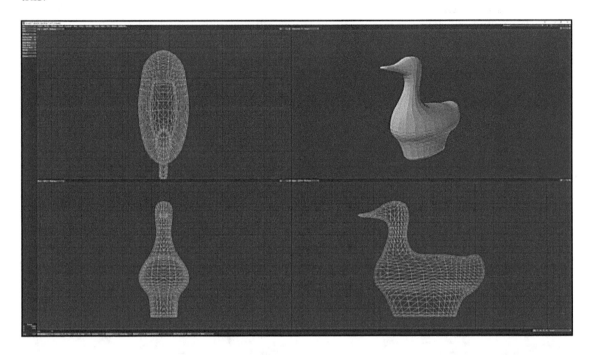

Booleans

Booleans are another function in any modeling tool. With these, you can join two pieces of geometry or even use one object to cut another. For example, consider the following diagram:

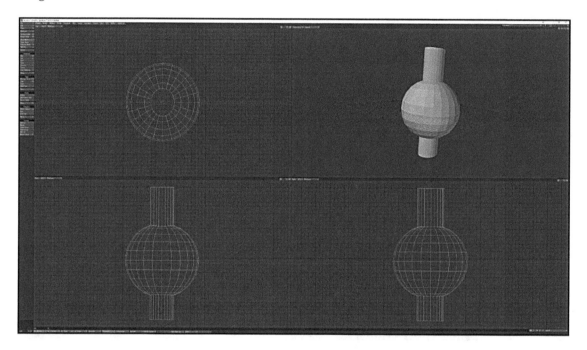

In the preceding diagram, we have a ball and a cylinder that have been combined into one object. Notice that there is no cylinder geometry inside the ball. It's one solid object. Whereas, in the following diagram, we have that same ball and cylinder, but the cylinder has been used to cut a hole in the ball. This is done by creating two objects and using the `Boolean` function:

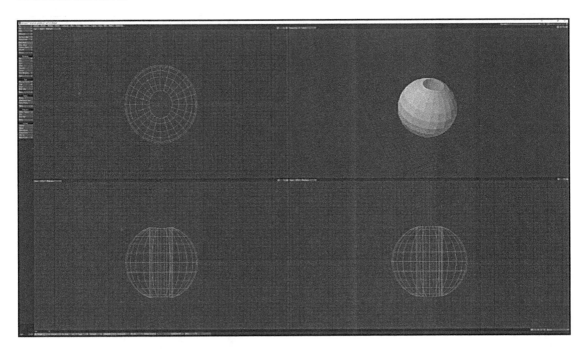

This method is how we created not just an access hole, but the lid on our duck. We simply created a basic shape, and used it once to cut (Boolean subtract) a hole. Then, we used that shape and the original duck again to create a lit (using Boolean intersect). Here, you can see them shown in different colours (as shown in the following diagram):

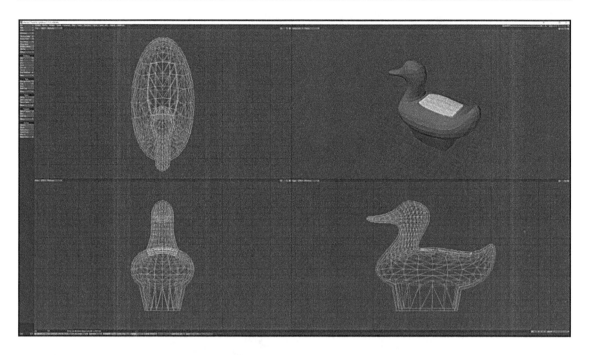

And there you have it—all the basic tools you need to model your own objects. Direct from your imagination to the real world—speaking of bringing them into the real world.

Printing large 3D models

Our duck is nearly 11-inches long. Our 3D printer has a 5.5 x 5.5-inch print bed. This means that we're going to have to print it in sections. Using the `Boolean` method (as we did earlier), we can cut our object into sections. But since this object is going to need to be water-tight, how do we do this?

Cyanoacrylate adhesives (**CA**) glue (basically, superglue) melts plastic together. It's great stuff. It's more like welding plastic than gluing it. So, in step one, we put a nice bead of glue on one of the two objects to be glued, and then just press them together for about 10 seconds. The glue dries up very fast. Just do yourself a favour, and don't touch the glue. Superglue is famous for bonding to skin (military medics and some surgeons use it to seal wounds).

Then, there are sure to be gaps in the joint. This is a problem. It happens because (although 3D prints are fairly precise) 3D prints can have small irregularities for a plethora of reasons. Sometimes, they can even warp slightly. We'll need to seal this all up. To do this, we put a large bead of silicone sealant over the entire joint, and then smooth it over with our finger. Use a surgical glove, or this can get messy. You can see the joined parts in the following image:

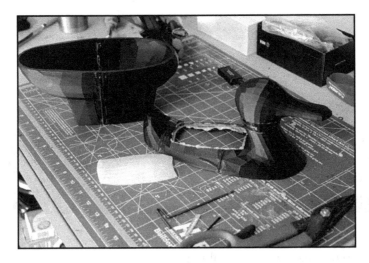

We're going to wait until we have the motor, prop, shaft, and electronics done to put on the top half of the duck. You can see that the top-half consists of four sections (not including the lid), and the bottom-half was done in two sections.

You may also notice a bead of silicone around the area for the lid-hole. This was a makeshift O-ring. We created this by covering the edges of the lid with petroleum jelly. Silicone will not stick to this. Then we put a bead on the black part (the top-half of the duck), and pressed the lid into it. This created a custom-moulded O-ring made of silicone once it dried. After the silicone dried, the lid popped right out. Now we have a water-tight seal for our lid! It's not as pretty as it could be... but it'll definitely work for our prototype.

Testing for water-tightness

As we mentioned earlier, we are going to test for water-tightness at every stage of construction. This is just done by filling a sink with water, and putting the part of the model into the water until the water, is nearly at the lip, for a minute or two. We look carefully for any sign of water coming through the model. You can see this in the following image with the bottom-half of the duck before adding the ballast clay.

It's important to not only let the silicone sealant dry, but let it cure for at least 24 hours before doing this:

After the success of this test, we fill the ballast section with modeling clay, and do it again for two reasons:

1. We want to make sure we didn't pack it with too firm a hand (breaking a seal)
2. We need to make sure that the water line comes up to the right level

The bottom-half with the clay pack is shown in the following image:

Awesome! Now that our duck is packed with 2 lbs of clay, we're sure that there's no way it's going to capsize. Also, now that we're sure that the duck is watertight, let's drill some holes in it! Wait... what?!

Installing the propulsion system

We want to perform the next steps before the clay dries up. First, we want to take out a small chunk of the clay at the back, and drill a hole at an angle. There, we'll feed the sleeve and drive shaft through and install the propeller. Do not ever glue a sleeve into place. It needs to remain flexible. Instead, we use a liberal amount of silicone to hold it in place, and seal the hole inside and out of the body (as shown in the following image):

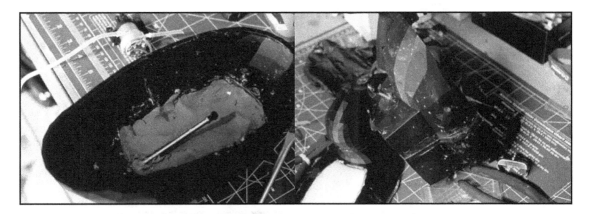

Now, it's time to make our motor mount. We wanted to see exactly where the drive shaft will be, the angle it's at, and where the hookup to the motor is. We do the same thing we did for the drive-shaft sleeve on the front of the boat. There, we put the long end of the water-cooling tube. We do this before placing the motor mount, because otherwise we wouldn't be able to get at it. This tube will take in water for the water cooling (as shown in the following image). After waiting for the silicone to dry, we can trim it back a bit but not flush:

After placing the motor mount (printed with ABS plastic), we glue the motor in (still using its mounting bracket from the original boat), and route the short end of the water-cooling tube out the side (as shown in the following image):

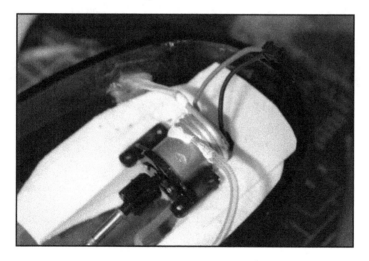

Steering and electronics

You may notice from the preceding image that the motor only has two-wires. This is because it's a brushed motor. In the last chapter, we discussed brushed versus brushless motors. A brushed motor requires an entirely different type of ESC. Why is this important? Because (unfortunately) the receiver for our original boat had an integrated ESC. So, we'll need to dig out a new brushed ESC for our motor. While the intern is doing that, let's install our newly printed rudder.

First, we created a block that fits on the back of our duck with the male end of a hinge on it. Then, a simple rudder with a control arm on it (so that as the servo pushes a control rod, the rudder will turn). Mounted, it looks like the following image:

On the inside, we glued our electronics platform into place, drilled a hole (well above the water line) for our control rod. The rod can't be encumbered by silicone, so this hole will leak if water rises to this line. So, we wanted it as high as possible. And we mounted our electronics platform (as shown in the following image):

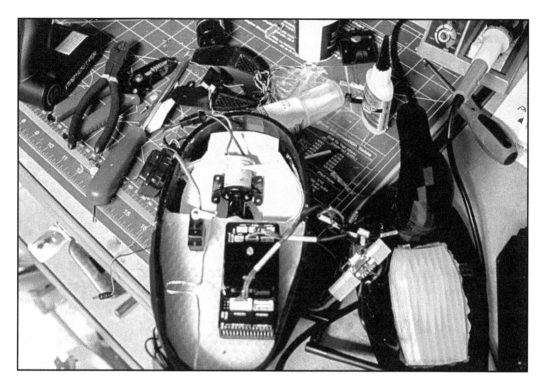

You can also see that we mounted our Pixhawk on the electronics platform. We put a bend in the control rod so that we can adjust its effective length to trim out our controls once everything is powered on.

Hooking everything up!

Well, do that after you've water tested it. The only thing worse than water on electronics is water on electronics when they have power! As for the plugs and hook-ups, everything works exactly the same as it did with the land rover. Instead of a servo to the wheels, it's one to the rudder. Instead of a motor to the wheels, it's on the propeller. But every plug should go in the same way on a water rover as with a land rover. Afterward, put the lid on, and program it the same exact way you did for the land rover. Then, you're off and swimming with the ducks!

Summary

In a book about Pixhawk drones, you may be asking, "Where's the programming of the Pixhawk?!" We'd be remiss in a book about designing purpose-built drones if we didn't cover something on the water. Plus, we want to show you that there are similarities between land and water drones. What we really wanted to get deeper into is the *design and prototyping* of an idea. Now that we've covered the modeling, and construction of your own design (we covered modeling, printing, water-sealing, design, sketching, identifying problems, and construction testing); in the next chapter, we're going to get much deeper into the Pixhawk.

We'll be taking a (pretty much) fully constructed vehicle (a motorized golf trolly), and adapting it for Pixhawk. We'll also be getting into using a mobile device (via Bluetooth) to control your drone, as well as getting deeper into the configuration of Pixhawk.

From here in, now that you're an expert in turning your construction designs into reality we're going to be focusing more on the Pixhawk device itself.

So, buckle up!

4
A Drone for Golfers

As we've stated a few times before, when choosing an industry to make a drone for, you have to balance the size of the market (demand), with how much money they have to spend (cost), and how easy it will be for you to fill that demand (supply).

One of the industries that is extremely popular is golf. Every year, consumers literally spend billions of dollars on golf equipment and accessories. One thing golfers go nuts about is the new technology to help their game. Sounds pretty much perfect, right?

So, where can a drone fit in? A multicopter to fly down the fairway and check the layout? Maybe, but if the golfer has played that course before, why would they need it? They wouldn't. Ok, that's a bad idea. What about a submarine drone to look for a golf ball that went into the water hazard? Not a terrible idea, but there are probably so many balls sitting at the bottom of a water hazard that finding your own ball may prove impossibly difficult. And who wants to keep pulling out golf balls that have been damaged by weeks of sitting at the bottom of a pond? Nope, another bad idea.

What's something that every professional golfer has, and every amateur wants (but may not be able to afford)? A caddy (someone to carry your clubs around the course)! So, what if we took a motorized golf trolly (a small cart that carries golf clubs) and made it follow a cell phone?

Now, we're on the right track.

We'll be covering the following topics:

- The design
- Using tank locomotion
- Using LIDAR to avoid obstacles

The design

After some initial research, we found that there is already such a device out on the market. It's called the *Stewart X9 Follow*. However, at a list price, this item is just shy of $3,000 US!

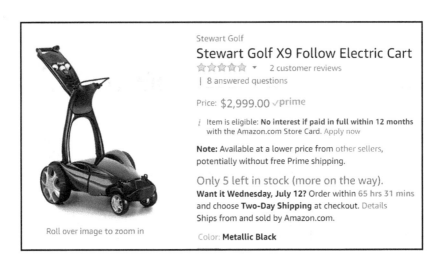

> Stewart Golf
> ### Stewart Golf X9 Follow Electric Cart
> ☆☆☆☆☆ ▾   2 customer reviews
> | 8 answered questions
>
> Price: **$2,999.00** ✓prime
>
> *i* Item is eligible: **No interest if paid in full within 12 months** with the Amazon.com Store Card. Apply now
>
> **Note:** Available at a lower price from other sellers, potentially without free Prime shipping.
>
> Only 5 left in stock (more on the way).
> **Want it Wednesday, July 12?** Order within 65 hrs 31 mins and choose **Two-Day Shipping** at checkout. Details
> Ships from and sold by Amazon.com.
>
> Roll over image to zoom in
>
> Color: **Metallic Black**

It's certainly a high-quality product—a very sleek and beautiful design. There is no doubt that the high-end golfer would love to indulge in this item. But for your average golfer, this would absolutely break the bank.

This item also uses its own remote. The rover follows the remote, or can be piloted manually with it. We're going to use a different approach. Instead of a proprietary remote, we'll make ours follow a smart phone (via Bluetooth or Wi-Fi). This means it can be paired easily. Also, we'll include a standardized RC remote (in the event that the user's phone runs out of battery because they forgot to charge it).

Using standardized parts should allow us to bring the final cost of our unit down to around $1,000 US. Our unit may not end up as luxurious as the Stewart, but it will hit a much wider section of the market.

Here's our original sketch:

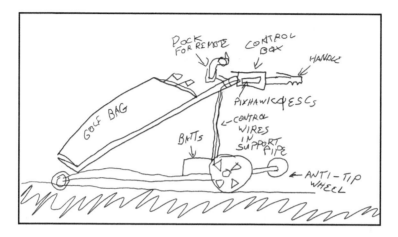

Fabricating an entire golf caddy could get quite expensive. So, let's start off with someone else's (already motorized) caddy. We found the following on Amazon:

The beauty of this trolley is that it already has dual motors (as it's built to be piloted via remote). All we really have to do is implement a *brain* in this *dumb* caddy. Then, it can intelligently follow a cell phone.

We are going to have to do a complete rewire to make this work though. The motors are brushed, so we're going to need two brushed ESCs. These speed controllers also need to be capable of reverse as well. Why? Because to turn the trolley, we will use a *tank* like steering (where one side goes forward and the other side reverses).

Now, we need to lay out exactly how everything will connect, so let's look at our wiring diagram:

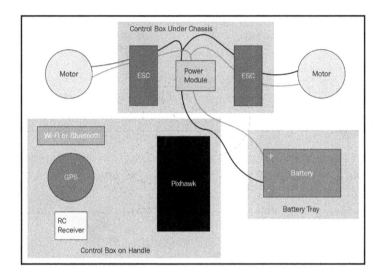

You may notice that we didn't include a **Battery Elimination Circuit** (**BEC**) to provide power to the servo section on the Pixhawk. That's because we're going to use ESCs that have BECs built in. This will provide voltage to the servo board via the ESC servo connections.

You'll also notice that at this juncture we hadn't decided whether to use Wi-Fi or Bluetooth as our communication protocol. We've eliminated the 900 Mhz data connection for laptops in favor of one of these protocols. Why? Because nobody's going to want to carry around a laptop on the golf course. Instead, we're going with a mobile device.

So, what's the difference? If we connect via Wi-Fi, the Pixhawk will become a network access point. This may actually present a problem because GPS requires a data connection on your phone to display maps. If we use Wi-Fi, the network is established with Pixhawk from your mobile device (rather than your service provider's cellular data connection).

If we use Bluetooth, we may have some issues with iOS devices. Only *Apple Approved* connections can be used in some cases. However, we can tackle that at a different point. For now, we're prototyping. So, for proof of concept, we'll use an Android mobile device and the Bluetooth protocol. Android is a bit easier to work with as a developer, and there are a plethora of Pixhawk control apps out for the platform. If worse comes to the worst, when we go to the market we could always include a basic android device with the trolley.

You can see from the wiring diagram how things fit together and where they go. We're not going to get deep into routing each wire and plugging everything in. You should be familiar with all that by now. This is where we get deeper into Pixhawk.

Using tank locomotion

Tank style locomotion is where there are no steerable wheels. Rather, wheels on one side of a vehicle move forward, while the wheels on the other side either stay stationary, or reverse (as illustrated in the following diagram). This is also called **skid-steering**:

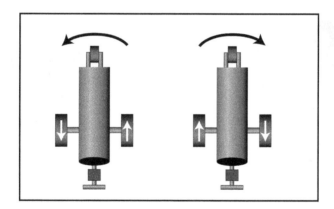

This kind of locomotion is great because vehicles can literally turn on a dime (in place). However, the drawback is that it can be *jerky* when turning while going forward. But as there's no sensitive equipment (just golf clubs), we don't really care if there's jostling of the clubs during turns. All we really want is to make this as inexpensive and simple as possible. You may notice that the front wheel is fixed (doesn't pivot as a caster would). This is of no concern to us as when steering occurs, the front wheel doesn't have a lot of weight on it (the center of gravity is right on top of the main wheels' axle). Therefore, the friction is minimal. If it turns out to be a problem, we can always replace the front wheel with a caster later.

So how do we make Pixhawk use a tank style drive system to steer the vehicle? Simple, really.

Adapting Pixhawk for skid-steering

The first thing is to plug the right ESC into the right port on the servo panel of the Pixhawk. The left wheel's ESC plugs into **MAIN OUTPUT 1**. The right wheel's ESC should go into **MAIN OUTPUT 3** as shown in the following diagram:

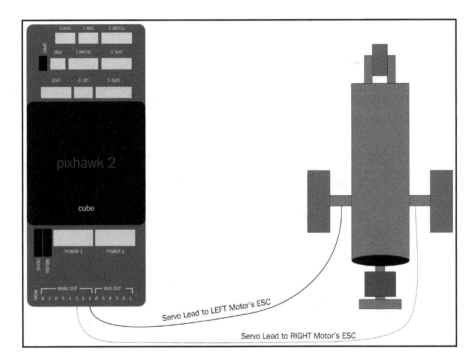

Now, we just have to enable skid-steering in the Pixhawk itself. It'll do all the work of figuring out what to do to what wheel all on its own!

Inside of the Mission Planner software, connect to the Pixhawk (after plugging in the USB cable of course). Enter the Config/Tuning screen and select **Standard Params** as shown in the following screenshot:

You'll notice that we highlighted two options in the preceding screenshot. These are the **SKID_STEER_IN** and **SKID_STEER_OUT** options. One of the great things about the Mission Planner's GUI is that it shows you what the options are that you're changing in the code. You could do the exact same thing we're doing with the code for Pixhawk if you simply searched for these options and changed what they are set to.

Notice that we set **SKID_STEER_IN** to None, and **SKID_STEER_OUT** to 1. Let's explain what these are, and why we set them to these values:

- **SKID_STEER_IN**: This is representative of just how the user will steer the tank. If they had two sticks on their remote, and wanted to steer by manually applying power to each track (for example, pulling the left stick back and pushing the right stick forward to turn left), you would want to set this option to 1. However, as we're using a steering wheel-style controller for our RC; we'll leave this set to None and let the Pixhawk do the throttle mixing for itself.
- **SKID_STEER_OUT**: This option is the switch to flip for whether or not we're using skid steering. For a normal RC rover with steerable wheels, we'd leave this set to None. But since we do want to use skid-steering, we'll set this to 1.

Now that we have our skid-steering set up, let's move on to setting up the Bluetooth data link so we can control it with a phone.

Using Bluetooth to control Pixhawk with a phone

Bluetooth with Pixhawk is a snap. But just like every other bit of Pixhawk functionality, an add-on module needs to be purchased. We picked up the one shown as follows:

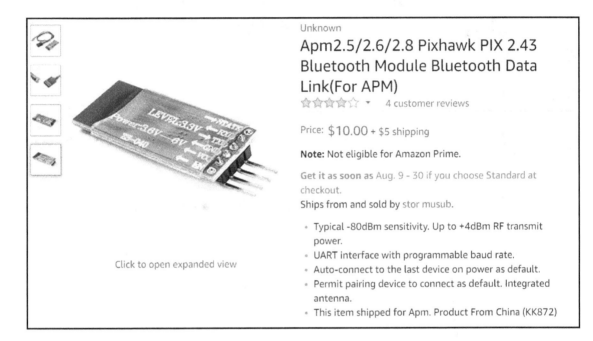

Unknown

Apm2.5/2.6/2.8 Pixhawk PIX 2.43 Bluetooth Module Bluetooth Data Link(For APM)

☆☆☆☆☆ ▾   4 customer reviews

Price: $10.00 + $5 shipping

Note: Not eligible for Amazon Prime.

Get it as soon as Aug. 9 - 30 if you choose Standard at checkout.

Ships from and sold by stor musub.

- Typical -80dBm sensitivity. Up to +4dBm RF transmit power.
- UART interface with programmable baud rate.
- Auto-connect to the last device on power as default.
- Permit pairing device to connect as default. Integrated antenna.
- This item shipped for Apm. Product From China (KK872)

Click to open expanded view

Of course, we had to alter the cable (just as we did before) because the cable included with this module is for the old-style plugs. We connected our Bluetooth module to the **Telem 1** port as shown in the following figure:

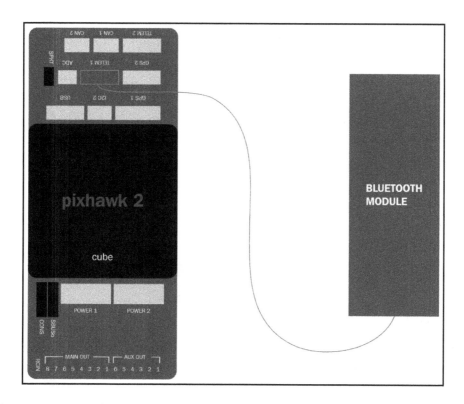

Now, it's just a matter of binding our Android device's Bluetooth to the Pixhawk's Bluetooth. Just power on your Pixhawk and bind using the same method you would for any Bluetooth device. The software to control Pixhawk from a mobile device is called **DroidPlanner 2**. It's free!

We're not quite there yet, but if you're curious on how to get a Pixhawk vehicle to follow you using DroidPlanner 2, it's easy! Just click on the **Follow** button, and set the radius you'd like the rover to stay within. Of course, you can ignore the `altitude` attribute (as this is a ground vehicle). You can see the **Follow** button in the following picture:

Of course, if you don't want the rover to follow you onto the putting green, just tap **Pause**. You can also click on the points on the map to send the rover off!

Pretty cool, huh? But what if there's a tree between you and your rover? You don't want it hitting trees and boulders while it's trying to get to you, right? Enter collision avoidance!

Using LIDAR to avoid obstacles

Would you like to go for a walk on a golf course blindfolded? No? Me neither, and it's probably not good to just set a rover to run around blind either. But vision and object recognition takes a lot more computing power than we're budgeted for on this machine. So, what's the next best thing to vision? SONAR or LIDAR. Unfortunately, SONAR (just like a bat finds insects using sound waves to calculate the distance to obstacles) is considered *passé* for Pixhawk, and thus the implementation is quite *wonky*. There are I2C sonar devices, but they don't work very well (if at all) with Pixhawk 2.1 and the latest Ardupilot firmware. So, we're going to use LIDAR instead. LIDAR rangefinders use light waves (instead of sound) to calculate the distance to objects.

LIDAR 101

LIDAR simply uses a light wave to send out, bounce off objects, and then looks for it to return. Since light travels at 299,792,458 m/s, all the LIDAR module has to do is measure the time it takes to return a light pulse back to the module. Bam! You can sense if there is an object and how far away it is. The following figure illustrates this:

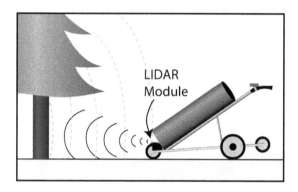

There are several different frequency, strength, and spread patterns for LIDAR. You may notice that we're planning on putting our LIDAR module on the top of the front fender. This is a perfect spot (as we'll be able to sense any objects too big for the front wheel to roll over! Let's talk about different aspects of LIDAR:

- **Rate**: This is how many times a second (also called Hz) a light pulse is generated and looked for. The unit we're using (Teraranger One) samples at a rate of 1000 Hz (1000 times a second). Fast rates are good, but if you're sensing for long-range contact, a longer time may be necessary (to avoid signals coming back at the same time, or even after the next signal is sent). Our 1000 Hz rate is fine though as our module has a range of 14 meters.
- **Range**: How far away the LIDAR will start detecting objects. Our sensor is rated for 14 meters. Considering our rover will be moving at a walking pace that's far more than enough range.
- **Resolution**: This parameter has to do with accuracy. The EZ4 we're using has a resolution of 0.5 cm. This means that it can tell the difference between 5.105 metres away from an object and 5.11 metres away from an object.
- **Width**: The width of the beam is also important. Our LIDAR module has a 3° wide beam. It should be effective enough to keep our rover out of too much trouble.

Making LIDAR work

Different LIDAR modules have different pin-outs (wiring scheme to the Pixhawk plug). Before you purchase a LIDAR module, you should check their compatibility on the Ardupilot website (`http://ardupilot.org/rover/docs/common-rangefinder-landingpage.html`). The wiring pin-outs and list of compatible sensors can be found there, as well as where to plug them in.

Mounting the module

The first step is deciding how you're going to mount your LIDAR. It should be pointed parallel to the ground (not up or down). If you are using a single sensor (as we are in this example), it should also be pointed straight ahead. If you're using several sensors, you want to place them in a way that they cover the whole area you wish the rover to see, but overlapping is not entirely necessary. The following diagram shows how we went about designing our sonar mounting option (we replaced the fender):

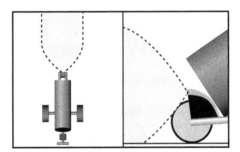

You can see that the diagram shows that the ground will overlap the pattern, so large rocks, roots, and fallen branches will be sensed. If we want to block some of the ground (so we can regulate just how big an obstacle will be noticed), all we have to do is slide the sensor back so that the fender blocks some of the ground. We doubt we'll need that though. Pixhawk has the ability to distinguish between the fender and objects further away (with a little tweaking).

Configuring LIDAR with Mission Planner

First, we need to tell Pixhawk that there is a rangefinder module before we start configuring it. So we plug Pixhawk into our computer (via USB), and initiate the connection from within Mission Planner.

In the **Initial Setup** section, you'll find **Optional Hardware**, and under that there will be **Range Finder**. In this section, you should choose the appropriate model of rangefinder you are using as shown in the following figure:

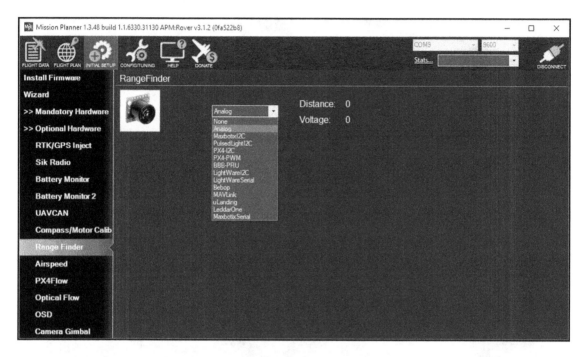

Newer versions of the Ardurover firmware have the Teraranger One in this dropdown menu. But if you're using an older version, you may need to set it in the **Full Parameter List**. This is done by opening Config/Tuning and selecting **Full Parameter List** from the left-hand side of the screen. The following is a list of the parameters, as well as their settings for the Teraranger One:

- **RNGFND_MAX_CM**: 1400 (14 m). This is the maximum range of the rangefinder in centimeters.
- **RNGFND_MIN_CM**: 20 (20 cm). This is the closest that the rangefinder will read objects.
- **RNGFND_TYPE**: 4. A numerical value that indicates this is an I2C LIDAR rangefinder that is a Teraranger One.

Now, let's take a look at all of the parameters we can use to adjust the sonar rangefinder with Pixhawk:

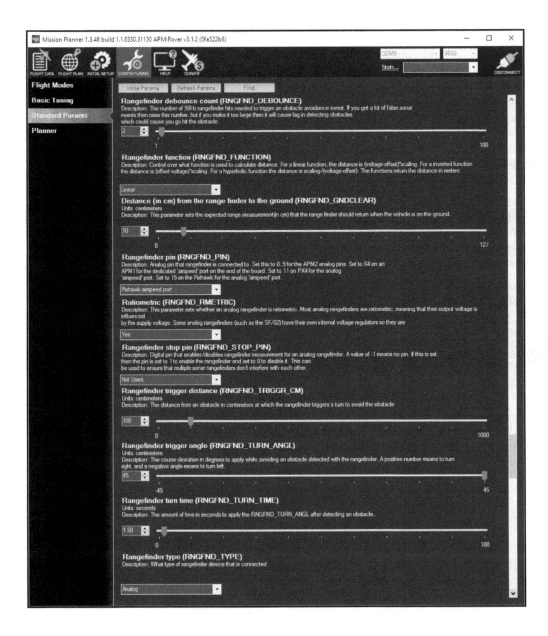

A lot of parameters, right? You got to love Mission Planner. There's a really good description beneath each option. But let's go ahead and explain these anyway:

- **RNGFND_DEBOUNCE**: These are a number of returned pings that an object needs to send back in order to be registered by Pixhawk. Why would you need this? Wider and longer range rangefinders can also generate more noise (or false pings). So, to make sure an object is really there you may need to increase this number to reduce false readings. But there's a catch—increasing this number also means it takes more time to register an object. This means that if you have a fast-moving drone you may not avoid the obstacle in time. Our LIDAR is very clear, so we'll leave this at the default of 2. This means that an object needs to return two consecutive pings to be registered by Pixhawk.
- **RNGFND_FUNCTION**: To understand this, you need to know that rangefinders return the distance to an object with a voltage ping, not a data ping. The rangefinder doesn't say, "Hey... it's 5 meters away." Instead, the rangefinder raises or lowers voltage sent back based on how strong a ping it receives. It's up to Pixhawk to interpret this. This setting determines how Pixhawk interprets voltage sent to it from a rangefinder.
- **RNGFND_GRNDCLEAR**: This function is mostly useful for planes and multicopters with downward-facing sonar. It indicates how far away the rangefinder is from the ground when an aircraft lands (the ground clearance of the module).
- **RNGFND_PIN**: This one may be a little confusing. Simply put, this is in reference to where voltage will be returned to the Pixhawk. You can leave this alone for the LIDAR we're using.

With a Teraranger, you shouldn't really need to play with any of these settings. One of the major selling points of the Teraranger is that it comes precalibrated. The one setting you're going to probably need to tune is the **RNGFND_DEBOUNCE** parameter. Seeing as the LIDAR module is so close to the ground, and that our rover is going to move at just about walking speed, we should set this up at 10. This means the module needs to receive 10 pings from an object before it recognizes that there is an object in its path. This will keep the noise from sticks, grass, and other objects down.

Now, let's check out the parameters that actually affect what the rover does when it detects an object:

- **RNGFND_TRIGGER_CM**: This is how far from an obstacle that Pixhawk will execute a turn (in centimeters) to avoid it. A value of 200 means 2 meters.
- **RNGFND_TURN_ANGL**: How many degrees that Pixhawk should make your rover turn to avoid an obstacle. A value of 45 means 45°. Using basic geometry (Pythagorean's theorem), Pixhawk will calculate when it is beyond the obstacle, and return to the course. Pixhawk will always attempt the turn in one direction; 45 means turn right 45° and -45 means turn left 45°.
- **RNGFND_TURN_TIME**: This is how many seconds to apply the turn. A value of 1.5 simply means to take 1.5 seconds to turn to the **RNGFND_TURN_ANGLE**.

When you put these all together, you can imagine the circumstances. Say you hit a golf ball off into some trees. Of course, your caddy follows you. It's moving at a normal walking pace of 3 MPH (or 1.34112 meters per second). Will 2 meters be enough to detect trouble? Yes, but a turn time of 1.5 seconds means that the cart will travel 2.012 meters before a turn completes. So, the `RNGFNG_TURN_TIME` is too long. Reduced to 1 second, and now we're down to 1.34112 meters again. That works with one tree. What if there are two? Or ten? A forest? It would probably be best to also increase our `RNGFND_TRIGGER_CM` to a more manageable and safe distance of 4000 (cm). That way, it's far less likely that our rover will turn into a tree while avoiding another.

Summary

In this chapter, we learned how to implement skid-steering, using a rangefinder for obstacle avoidance, and how to make a rover follow us using Bluetooth and an Android phone app. As you can see (on some) applications with Pixhawk can be far easier than they seem at first. You can pilot your rover with your phone and even use a map to lay out a course (using waypoints) for the rover to automatically drive itself. But, most importantly, your new rover will follow your phone as if it were on a leash.

Now, we'll move on to some more advanced applications for Pixhawk aircraft. Brace yourself, this is where designing, fabricating, and implementing Pixhawk gets a lot more complex. But it's also where Pixhawk really shines, and is a whole lot of fun!

5
Introduction to UAVs

UAVs are significantly different from rovers. They aren't tethered to the ground, have a greater range (generally), and are far more dangerous to work with. Sounds exciting, right? In this chapter, we'll cover the complexities of designing an aerial drone. We'll talk about airframes, weight, flight time, and propulsion. Let's talk a bit about safety first, so we can make things a bit less exciting, okay?

We'll be covering the following topics:

- Safety concerns
- Propellers - flying cuisinarts!
- Designing for air and ground
- Learning some physics
- Designing a multicopter airframe
- Designing a fixed wing-airplane)

Safety concerns

Before even considering designing an aerial drone, you first need to figure out a testing ground. As an example, I'll show you what I use, but before we get into that, let's talk about the requirements you should look for:

1. **Authorized for RC air traffic**: An **Academy of Model Aeronautics** (**AMA**-
   http://www.modelaircraft.org/) authorized flying field is a good place to start
   with. You know that RC aircraft are okay in the area if there is such a flying field.
   If there isn't one in your area, the next place to look is at FAA charts. You can find
   current online charts at SkyVector (https://skyvector.com/). These charts will
   show all restricted airspace. Anything unrestricted is okay to fly RC aircraft.

2. **Remote**: Just because an area allows RC aircraft does not mean it's safe to test a new aircraft (especially an autonomous one). You'll need to make sure that there aren't any major buildings, homes, or pedestrians in the area that could get damaged (or even killed) if it crashes or decides to fly away. With the instructions we give you in the following chapters, everything should work. But unfortunately, we don't live in the world of what should be.

3. **You are authorized to be there**: Don't go trespassing on someone's ranch to test out your aircraft. At best, you could get in some legal trouble. At worst (in some places) you may even get shot. It's always good to ask for permission from the owner if you're going onto private property.

With these requirements in mind, the following Google Maps images show an example of a bad flying field (left) versus a good flying field (right). The one on the left is A-Main Hobbies' flying field in Chico, CA-great for recreational flying; completely wrong for prototyping. The one on the right is Dick Scobee Airfield in George Bush Park in Houston, TX-in the middle of a giant park. This is not perfect (because there is a road running through it), but definitely doable:

The one on the right is where I generally fly nowadays (since moving out to Texas). The one on the left is where I flew (already vetted aircraft) when I lived in California. For testing, I had to drive several hours to a remote location.

Propellers - flying cuisinarts

Try not to allow onlookers when you're testing. Here's an incident that happened with me in 2009:

I was testing a new design of a multicopter (heavy-lift octocopter), and moments after I plugged in the battery, it took off with no warning. The blades literally chewed up my shins and knees, and then the multicopter tilted and started heading for my kids (who really wanted to see Daddy's new aircraft fly). Despite the pain and gushing blood, I managed to dive for the multicopter, grab it, and throw it to the ground in return breaking the blades. Luckily, it worked. But because I wanted to show off to my kids, they could have been scarred for life! To this day, I wear shorts on set to show the scars to people who don't take safety around multicopters seriously.

The moral of that story? My kids should have never been there to begin with. When experienced pilots talk about safety, or the AMA comes out with safety advisements, these are based on experience. Experience that is better learned from someone else, and not first hand.

Here are some general practices you should follow when testing:

- **Keep onlookers away**: Sometimes it's unavoidable though. You may have investors, or just people you can't get rid of. In this case, keep them behind you. It's safe to say that you'll do everything possible to avoid hitting yourself. But if you do, hospital bills are cheaper than lawsuits!
- **Perform inspections before every flight**: Whether you're prototyping or even using a tried and true platform, things can come loose from vibration. Parts can bend or even get small fractures. Just because nothing went wrong on your last flight, doesn't mean nothing will go wrong on the next flight. Also, you should check your battery level with a tester before putting it in the aircraft. Furthermore, you should always check weather conditions before each flight.
- **Test your controls with no propellers**: Your initial preflight of the day should include a test of all controls (including throttle). Take the propeller(s) off before you test!
- **Test in small increments**: Don't just take off and try to fly right away. If you're using a fixed-wing (airplane) with landing gear, taxi it around on the runway for a bit. Don't ever try autonomous flight on your first day. Basically, use some common sense. Get your controls dialled in so that you're making no compromises before moving on to the next test, and test several times at each stage.

- **Don't ever push a bad situation**: If a test isn't working, shut it down immediately! Fix the problem, and then try again.

Basically, have some respect for the dangers with an unproven aircraft, and use some common sense!

Designing for air versus ground

Air is an entirely different beast from ground (or water) design. Everything affects the way an aerial drone flies. We mean literally everything. Let us take a look.

Weight

Weight doesn't just affect the ability of a drone to get airborne. That much is obvious. Let's take an example from my experience. In the following image, you'll see a monster-sized fixed wing drone (the Skywalker X-8) with a nearly 8-foot wingspan, sitting on a slingshot-style launcher (known as a jetapult):

I built this drone in 2011. I thought I was really smart. The maximum payload for takeoff is 3.2 kg. So, I packed it full of batteries because I wanted this drone to stay in the air for extended periods of time. It flew beautifully when I was on the sticks. The first time I tested it on autonomous flight, the wings (literally) blew right off the plane, and it turned into a very expensive lawn-dart. It was completely totalled. So, what happened?

I failed to take into account g-force. G-force is the force put on an object due to centrifugal force. It is measured in multiples of the standard gravity of the Earth when standing still, on the ground, at sea level. For instance, a 100 lb pilot taking a 2-G turn will weigh 200 lbs during that turn.

When I flipped a switch for the plane to return home, it accelerated to maximum throttle, banked to 45 degrees, and took a tight turn to come back home. This was probably a good 4-G turn. So, even though I was under the weight limit at takeoff (only 3.0 kg), during that turn the aircraft had forces of 12.0 kg put directly on the wings. This was enough to shatter the wings and begin the metamorphosis to lawn-dart. A very stupid, expensive, and easy oversight to make.

Weight can also affect flight time. This is much more severe with multicopters because multicopters use power to generate lift, but it's also true with fixed-wing drones. Why? Because weight affects your glide ratio. The glide ratio of a plane looks something like 1:100. This means that for every 100 feet of forward flight, it will lose 1 foot of altitude with no power. To overcome this, the nose is ever-so-slightly pointed up and power is applied. Increase the weight, and the distance a plane will travel before losing altitude with no power will decrease; therefore, increase the weight and increase the power that is necessary to keep the plane airborne. And therefore, the less flight time you will have before exhausting your power supply.

A multicopter's glide ratio is 1:0. This means it can't travel forward at all without losing altitude without power. Essentially, it's even less of a glide ratio than a piano. So weight greatly affects the flight time of a multicopter. We'll get deeper into that when we build a multicopter in `Chapter 6`, *A Simple Multicopter Drone*.

Finally, weight also affects the **center of gravity** (**cg**). Flying an aircraft is a bit like balancing a ball on the point of a pencil. An aircraft should be as balanced as possible to enable the control surfaces to work properly with the most efficiency (fixed wing), or to keep the motors from being out of balance, and potentially burning out one of them (on a multicopter). Either way, an unbalanced aircraft will handle poorly, to say the least.

On a fixed-wing aircraft, you may find that the cargo compartment (where battery, electronics, and payload are kept) is on the front of the airframe. Put too much too far forward, and you'll find that the center of gravity becomes nose-heavy. This means you may need to add more weight to the tail as ballast (counterweight). Generally, the cg for a fixed-wing aircraft is on the peak of the airfoil. Think of this as a fulcrum on a scale. You'll need to balance that scale. We'll get deeper into this in two chapters when we build a fixed-wing aircraft.

Power/lift

There was a time when having a multicopter stay in the air for more than 5 minutes was considered a feat of engineering.

One of my multicopters from the past was built for small camcorders (barely larger than a GoPro). It's pictured next, as featured in Videomaker Magazine. I was asked by a client to mount a Blackmagic Cinema camera on it. Of course, it was designed to lift that much weight. But for how long? It only stayed in the air for a whopping 2 minutes at a time. Power and lift need to be carefully balanced with the weight and battery to keep (especially) a multicopter in the air:

Fuel - battery

The simplest way to get more flight time is to add bigger batteries or more fuel, right? Wrong! If your drone is gas-powered, you have to keep in mind that fuel weighs 8 lbs per gallon and batteries give diminishing returns. For instance, using a battery that can power your motors 1X spec may weigh 2 lbs. But going to 2X spec may weigh 6 lbs. So twice the power rating on a battery doesn't mean twice the time because the motors have to work 3X as hard to keep that extra weight in the air!

Learning some physics

Nooooo! (you're probably saying). Unfortunately, depending on what you're prototyping, kitbashing may not be much of an option. Because we are going to kitbash in our chapters (as we could write a whole other book per type of aircraft), let's give you a brief crash course in aeronautical engineering.

Designing an aircraft from scratch is not for the faint of heart. Multicopters are much easier, so let's cover that first.

Designing a multicopter airframe

What, what in the heck is an airframe? It's just a fancy word for the body of an aircraft. Why would you need to design your own? Well, if you're going to start a new company selling a saturated product (such as a camera drone), you may need to differentiate yourself with an entirely new-looking drone. After all, why would anybody buy your design on (say) a DJI airframe, when they can just go buy a DJI?

Designing a multicopter frame is fairly easy; there are just a few factors you need to take into account, which we will cover in the upcoming subsections.

Symmetry

Keeping the motors driving the propellers equidistant is very important. Remember, a multicopter can fly in any direction equally well. To keep this important aspect of a multicopter, you must design your multirotor with motors in this pattern.

Even numbers

There is an exception, namely tricopters (three rotors). Although these were fairly common about 5 years ago, they are notoriously unstable. Why? Because of how multicopters turn. More blades not only equal better stability and lift for a multicopter, even numbers make the calculations necessary for Pixhawk to keep it in the air easier. If you remember, back in Chapter 1, *Drones 101*, we covered the physics of how a multicopter's yaw works. Even numbers make this far more stable.

In conjunction with symmetry, let's lay out how many degrees the different blade configurations would be in the following table. Just imagine looking at the multicopter from before and dividing the sections like slicing a pie. If there are 360 degrees in a circle, here's how things would line up:

Number of rotors	Degrees of separation
3	120
4	90
6	60
8	45

Blade clearance

The spars you design (the sticks that go from the center of the aircraft out to the motors) need to be long enough so that the blades clear any antennae and clear each other comfortably. So the more rotors that you have, the longer the spars need to be. The longer the spars are, the stronger they also need to be (due to the force known as **leverage**). Then, you have to understand that the longer and stronger the spars, the more weight you add in airframe and wiring for the motors.

With all of the preceding factors in mind, here is an example of an 8-rotor multicopter (octocopter) with 22-inch propellers:

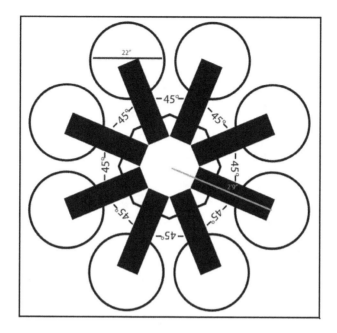

Here, you can see that each spar is 45° from each other, and each rotor is 2'9" from the center of the airframe to the center of the rotor. Add another 22", and you have a full blade-span of 4'7". Yes, it's a biggie. You may also notice that each spar is shorter than the exact center of each rotor. This is to allow for a motor-mount that is designed to fit in, using a sleeve, over the spar.

The math on airframes is easy. Just make the spars long enough so the blades have some clearance (and don't cause a ton of turbulence for each other), set the motors at symmetrical points around the center, and use even numbers of rotors. Personally, I don't advise tricopters. They are inherently unstable because they have an odd number of rotors.

There's a lot more that goes in if you want to get fancy (changing the angle of the rotors to assist with turning, thrust, and so on). But these are the basics.

Designing a fixed wing - airplane

Buckle up, because this is rocket science. Airplanes need to keep moving forward to stay in the air. We want as little wind resistance (drag) as possible when designing an airplane. This will let it stay in the air longer and relieve some stress on our motor.

There are hundreds of design motifs for airplanes, but let's use the three major ones (as shown in the following diagram):

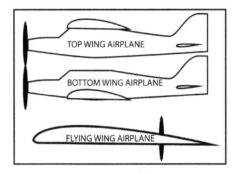

If the flying wing style is confusing, take a quick look back at the picture of the Skywalker X-8. That is a flying wing. Here's an example of a jet-propelled drone I'm currently designing, which is also a flying wing. It uses **Electric Ducted Fan** (**EDF**) jets rather than propellers to keep it going:

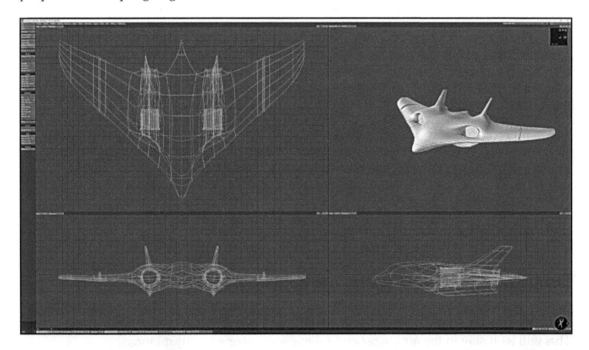

Obviously, this one is meant to go fast, very fast. But using EDF jets has a tradeoff-very short flight times and very high battery consumption. So, we'll stick with propellers.

The advantages and disadvantages with these designs are explained as follows:

- **Top wing**: This design is the easiest to make. It's also the most forgiving of design problems. If you design your own airplane, this is probably the design you should choose your first time out. All of the weight is below the wing, so it naturally wants to remain upright.
- **Bottom wing**: The biggest advantage of this design is the possibility of putting retractable landing gear onboard. Generally, the side gear would retract into the wings. However, as most of the weight is over the wing, it is a bit less stable and less forgiving of design errors.
- **Flying wing**: Flying wings are by far the design that can lift the most and stay in the air far longer. Their whole body is part of the wing. Therefore, very little surface area (all of which generates drag) isn't devoted to lift. However, they are by far the least forgiving of design problems. They also afford the ability to easily design in some retractable landing gear.

Pretty obvious and easy so far, right? Well, let's get to the difficult parts now.

Wing design

Ready to bone up on your math? Because here are the equations involved in airfoil (wing) design:

	Front $(0 \leq x < r)$	Back $(r \leq x \leq 1)$
Camber (standard)	$y_c = \dfrac{k_1}{6}\left(x^3 - 3rx^2 + r^2(3-r)x\right)$	$y_c = \dfrac{k_1 r^3}{6}(1-x)$
Gradient (standard)	$\dfrac{dy_c}{dx} = \dfrac{k_1}{6}\left(3x^2 - 6rx + r^2(3-r)\right)$	$\dfrac{dy_c}{dx} = \dfrac{k_1 r^3}{6}$
Camber (reflex)	$y_c = \dfrac{k_1}{6}\left((x-r)^3 - \dfrac{k_2}{k_1}(1-r)^3 x - r^3 x + r^3\right)$	$y_c = \dfrac{k_1}{6}\left(\dfrac{k_2}{k_1}(x-r)^3 - \dfrac{k_2}{k_1}(1-r)^3 x - r^3 x + r^3\right)$
Gradient (reflex)	$\dfrac{dy_c}{dx} = \dfrac{k_1}{6}\left(3(x-r)^2 - \dfrac{k_2}{k_1}(1-r)^3 - r^3\right)$	$\dfrac{dy_c}{dx} = \dfrac{k_1}{6}\left(3\dfrac{k_2}{k_1}(x-r)^2 - \dfrac{k_2}{k_1}(1-r)^3 - r^3\right)$

UGH, right? Luckily, there is a free online tool for just about everything (including plotting the profile of an airfoil you design). Airfoil tools (`http://airfoiltools.com/plotter/index`) is a great place to figure out the airfoil shape for your wing from a profile. A generated airfoil looks like the following image:

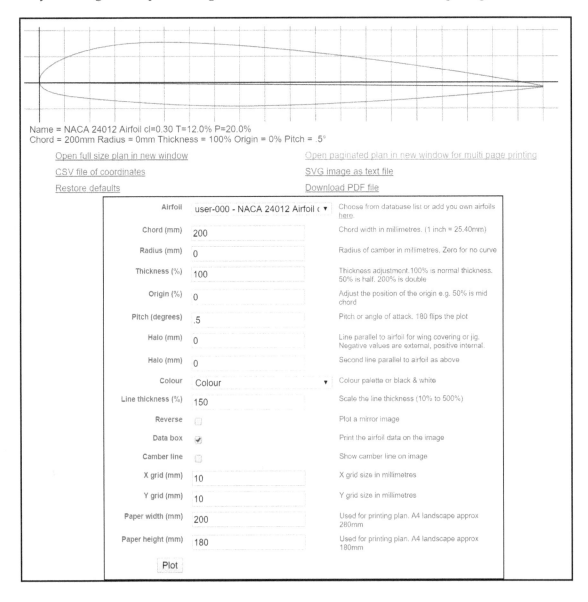

Name = NACA 24012 Airfoil cl=0.30 T=12.0% P=20.0%
Chord = 200mm Radius = 0mm Thickness = 100% Origin = 0% Pitch = .5°

Open full size plan in new window   Open paginated plan in new window for multi page printing

CSV file of coordinates   SVG image as text file

Restore defaults   Download PDF file

Airfoil	user-000 - NACA 24012 Airfoil ▼	Choose from database list or add you own airfoils here.
Chord (mm)	200	Chord width in millimetres. (1 inch = 25.40mm)
Radius (mm)	0	Radius of camber in millimetres. Zero for no curve
Thickness (%)	100	Thickness adjustment. 100% is normal thickness. 50% is half. 200% is double
Origin (%)	0	Adjust the position of the origin e.g. 50% is mid chord
Pitch (degrees)	.5	Pitch or angle of attack. 180 flips the plot
Halo (mm)	0	Line parallel to airfoil for wing covering or jig. Negative values are external, positive internal.
Halo (mm)	0	Second line parallel to airfoil as above
Colour	Colour ▼	Colour palette or black & white
Line thickness (%)	150	Scale the line thickness (10% to 500%)
Reverse	☐	Plot a mirror image
Data box	☑	Print the airfoil data on the image
Camber line	☐	Show camber line on image
X grid (mm)	10	X grid size in millimetres
Y grid (mm)	10	Y grid size in millimetres
Paper width (mm)	200	Used for printing plan. A4 landscape approx 280mm
Paper height (mm)	180	Used for printing plan. A4 landscape approx 180mm
Plot		

Even with this tool in place, it's still a bit confusing, right? Let's talk about these parameters and what they mean:

- **Chord (mm)**: Simply put, it's the entire length of your airfoil. It's the straight line from the front tip to the back tip.
- **Radius (mm)**: This is the radius of the curve used to generate the very front curve on the airfoil (the leading edge).
- **Thickness (%)**: This is the vertical measurement at the thickest part of the wing.
- **Origin (%)**: This has zero impact on the airfoil shape. It just moves the origin point of the grid backward from the nose of the wing.
- **Pitch (degrees)**: This is how much the overall design of the wing is pitched up from being level.
- **Halo (mm)**: This involves zero impact on the airfoil shape. It just draws a line inside or outside of the outer line to help if you're using this image to cut with a jig.
- **All other parameters**: This is also just for how the airfoil is drawn for your plans from grid size to paper size.

See? It's not really that bad. It sure is a heck of a lot harder than a multicopter though, and the development cycle is much much longer. You'll need to test fly the airplane several times and tweak the design until you're happy (long before implementing Pixhawk).

Summary

In this chapter, you got a good primer for all that is involved in designing an aircraft and the differences between an aircraft and a rover. I'm sure now you can see why we started with rovers. Compared to the aircraft, they're a piece of cake.

In the next chapter, we'll be showing you how to implement Pixhawk into a multicopter. We won't be focusing on designing a multirotor so much as making it work. So, we'll kitbash a DJI Flamewheel F550 airframe. Enjoy!

6
A Simple Multicopter Drone

Multicopters are very complex beasts. An awful lot can be done with Pixhawk and multicopters. Through the programming interface **Micro Air Vehicle Link** (**MAVLink**), all sorts of missions can be triggered automatically. From an alarm system trigger sending a drone out to a specific waypoint (based on the sensor triggered), to missions that adjust to varying conditions such as weather, light conditions, or any other number of variables only limited by your imagination—multicopters are the most versatile, yet complex, systems available for your design and concepts.

For the purposes of this book, we're going to keep things simple though. Once you're ready to take the leap into programming full applications for the MAVLink interface, there are great tutorials and a full coding guide at the *QgroundControl* website (`http://www.mavlink.org/dev/mavlink_groundcontrol_integration_tutorial`).

What we're going to do is show you how to design one of the most complex machines that Pixhawk can control—multicopter drone. Specifically, we're going to show how to design and prototype a 360 VR video multicopter.

What is 360 VR video, and why make a drone for it?

A 360 VR video is exactly what it sounds like: a camera that shoots video across 360° in every direction (a full sphere). It allows a user wearing VR goggles (such as Oculus Rift) to look in any direction during the playback of the video (rather than being restricted to a single field of view with traditional cameras). Also, phones and other mobile devices can be used to view 360 video by moving the device (like a window into the VR world) in any direction. Pretty cool, huh?

Since early humans looked to the sky and saw their first bird, we've dreamed of flight. From Superman to Jessica Jones, people have capitalized on people's idolization of flight. So, why not us? With 360 VR video in the air, we can take people into the air, and let them fly. With some special software in postproduction, the drone can even be removed from the picture giving the wearer of a VR headset a fully immersive experience in flight without looking out a window.

But before spending tens to hundreds of thousands of dollars on a high-end camera, and heavy lift drone, we need a proof of concept. That's where we come in.

Spec-ing out the parts

We know we want something stable that can fly for decent periods of time. So it should be easy, right? Wrong. We can't just buy a Phantom and stick a 360 camera on it. The footage will be unstable. So we'll need something that has (what's known as) a gimbal on it. A camera gimbal (usually) uses brushless motors to counteract the tilt of a multirotor vehicle. Multirotors (as we said before) tilt to travel in different directions. We don't want our camera tilting along with it. Otherwise, every course correction will send viewers tilting and twitching in all sorts of ways. We want very smooth footage. You can see what a camera gimbal looks like in the following image:

Of course, our proof of concept gimbal won't be anything near this elaborate but the principle of their operation is the same. We need something to dampen vibration, and counter the constant tilting and rolling of a multicopter.

But we're getting a bit ahead of ourselves. What's a nice, inexpensive camera we can use to do some 360 VR video on a proof of concept?

Starting with the payload

The drone is just a delivery device for its payload, in this case, a camera. So, it makes sense when designing any drone to start with what it is that you're trying to carry. On any proof of concept, the idea is to spend as little money as possible to prove your concept. Just start with the assumption that you will encounter problems and maybe even crashes (especially with a multicopter). Why risk a $10,000 camera (or even a $1,000 camera) on a proof of concept? Start small, and then scale up!

So, we found the perfect camera—a Ricoh Theta S. The Theta S is small, lightweight, has an integrated (built-in) battery, and an integrated memory card. The less we have to worry about, the better right? Best of all, it shoots in the same 360 format as any high-end 360 camera, and only costs $326! It's quite simply the goPro of 360 Cameras. The Amazon listing for the Theta S is shown in the following screenshot:

Ricoh

Ricoh Theta S Digital Camera (Black)

☆☆☆☆☆ ▾ · 427 customer reviews

| 173 answered questions

Price: **$326.95** ✓prime

In Stock.

Want it Tuesday, Aug. 1? Order within 3 hrs 50 mins and choose **Two-Day Shipping** at checkout. Details
Ships from and sold by Amazon.com. Gift-wrap available.

Style: **Base**

- 360 Degree Spherical Panorama images and Spherical Videos up to 25 minutes
- Live view function on mobile device
- Transfer videos directly to your mobile device without the need of a computer
- Full HD Video at 30fps
- 360 Degree Spherical Video Supported by YouTube

Roll over image to zoom in

Also, (as you can see on the listing), we already owned one! Always try to use things already in your shop for proof of concept. It saves a lot of cash! We purchased ours the previous summer to do some prototyping of our 360 VR editing workflow in postproduction.

The problem we'll now encounter is that (most) gimbals (especially inexpensive ones) are made for goPros. Some more expensive ones can be balanced for any camera... but they are meant for much bigger and heavier cameras. We don't want to invent an all new gimbal for our drone. That's not our business and is way beyond our scope for this proof. So, how do we manage a Theta S on an existing gimbal for our proof of concept?

Choosing the gimbal

As we've already said, the gimbal's main purpose is to keep the camera stable. It does this with the help of two methods:

1. Dampen vibration through rubber grommets (between the main frame and the gimbal mount).
2. Counter the normal tilting, rolling, and yaw movement of the drone via brushless motors on each axis.

Vibration dampening, we're all good. The same grommets are used for huge cameras as the smallest (just the count of grommets may change). Where our difficulty lies is in the balancing of the gimbal itself. We'd like to use a goPro gimbal (as it's nearly the same weight—125 grams for the Theta S and 149 grams for the goPro). Although the Theta S is (technically) lighter, the weight distribution will be completely different. It's a long, thin camera (that we'll likely have to hang upside down). But, because the dimensions are completely different, we can't ignore the principle of leverage on the gimbal axis. Remember give me a lever long enough, and I can move the world?

We'll need to make sure that our gimbal can overcome the extra (effective) weight due to leverage, and keep our Theta S stable. This means it'll also need to be somewhat programmable to keep it properly calibrated.

Finally, we'll need to make sure it's inexpensive. So, off to Amazon we go and this is what we arrived at:

FeiyuTech

Feiyu Tech FY-M3D Mini 3D PRO 3-Axis Air Gimbal with 360 Degree Panning for GoPro (Black)

☆☆☆☆☆ ▾   152 customer reviews | 145 answered questions

Price: $169.99 ✓prime

Note: Available at a lower price from other sellers, potentially without free Prime shipping.

Only 9 left in stock - order soon.

Want it Tuesday, Aug. 1? Order within 21 mins and choose **Two-Day Shipping** at checkout. Details

Sold by SpaceMall and Fulfilled by Amazon. Gift-wrap available.

It has enough motor power to allow for the variances in weight distribution, and gives us the ability to program the controller via USB!!! So far, our total budget is up to $496.94 US. OK we're doing good for a proof of concept (so far).

Now, how will we mount the Theta S to this gimbal? Well, enter our 3D printers from the previous chapters. We use our calliper measuring device (once the gimbal arrives) to measure the actual goPro mount, as well as the dimensions of our Theta S (at its widest point). The Theta S is kind of football-shaped on its y-axis (height-wise). This works well for us.

If we design a mount that fits a goPro's dimensions, but has a gap in the center that is square, a simple bead of silicone on the sides of where the Theta S will be pinched in will make it very strong and have enough friction to keep the Theta in place. Here's the simple (and lightweight) design we worked up:

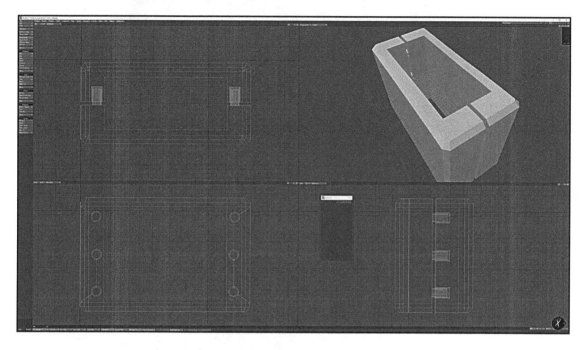

There are a few design elements that should stand out to you:

1. The edges are bevelled so that if any measurement (or 3D printing) variance will make the adapter seat firmly into the mount.
2. There are pins and holes so that the adapter holds the Theta S without the danger of the two sides of the clamshell sliding apart.
3. The hole for the Theta S to slip into is square (and not football shaped).

Here is what the final 3D-printed adapter looks like:

It may be a bit difficult to see (as we also used transparent filament in our printer) the two beads of silicone sealant used on each half of the clamshell, but this is the reason it works so well. It offers a lot of traction, and is flexible enough to really put the squeeze on our Theta S. Also, notice that the 3D print is hollow with a honeycomb inside. This makes it nice and light, yet strong. Here's how it looks with the Theta S strapped in:

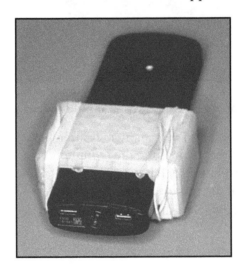

Seems immensely simple, right? It is. Sometimes the best solutions are. For proof of concept designs, sometimes rubber bands and zip ties are your best friends. You may be wondering if the rubber bands will interfere with the goPro mount. I assure you they won't. In fact, they'll come in handy. But we'll get there in the assembly stage.

So, our final weight is 146 grams, which is still less than a goPro. It's important to keep weighing things as you go with a multicopter. I apologize for the schmegged scale. It's also the scale we use to weigh silicone ingredients before mixing. But trust me, it was zeroed (with the Theta neoprene cover already on it) before the weight; 146g is accurate.

OK,, so far our total weight is 149 grams (gimbal) + 146 grams (camera) for a grand total of 295 grams. It's extremely important to keep track of weight while putting together an aerial drone (especially a multicopter). Now we just need a drone that can lift that payload and land safely.

Landing gear

Well, we're in a pickle here. The problem is that we need retractable landing gear (as shown in the following screenshot):

Why? We're working with 360 VR video here. We want to just replace the drone (and put in more sky) not have to rotoscope out landing gear on the sides and below our camera. But the landing gear wouldn't arrive for a month! Additionally, there's no real way to mount our gear and our gimbal to the drone. We need a rail system.

Enter the landing gear as shown in the following screenshot:

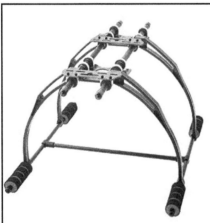

Ugh. Well, they don't retract, but they do have rails so, we'll order both. We'll put the rails on the drone, and run our basic flight tests. Then, when the retracts arrive, we'll be all set to run some video tests. It'll cost us an extra $20.99, but who cares? In the grand scheme of things, it's a drop in the bucket. We're also in a time crunch. So if the retracts don't arrive in time, we can still run some tests and get this thing in the air!

What's the biggest thing these two have in common? Lots of clearance. That way, the extra length of our camera and gimbal will still clear flat ground/a landing pad. It's by far the most important part to keep the camera safe.

So far, our total budget has reached $561.63 US. And we haven't even bought our airframe, motors, propellers, and ESCs yet. Luckily, we already have a Pixhawk.

But we're not at that point. Now, since we really have no way of previewing our 360 video (without using Wi-Fi) on this camera... we'll need a second FPV (first person view) camera (so we can see what's happening with our drone from the ground station). We never want to use Wi-Fi on an aerial platform. There's too much possibility of interference with control signals. That would be full risk and you never want to go full risk.

A first-person view – FPV system

In the US, it's illegal to fly a drone outside of **visual line of sight** (**VLOS**) without a special waiver. However, you're safest if when you look at a laptop screen, you can still see something about where your drone is headed, right? So an FPV system is a necessary safety feature (if used properly). Plus, it gives the director of your VR shoot an opportunity to see (first hand) where the drone is shooting from and direct you properly.

Since this is just a proof of concept, we don't need a very powerful system. It doesn't need a very long range, and as this is just a small version of a production drone it really needs to be as simple and light as possible.

Enter the (all in one unit) Spektrum FPV camera with an integrated transmitter:

That's another 85 grams, bringing our total weight (so far) up to 295 grams + 200 grams (landing gear + rails) + 85 grams (camera/transmitter) = 580 grams. See how it just keeps getting bigger and bigger? But wait, there's more!

This transmitter works at a much smaller voltage than our drone. We have two options: either put in some sort of transformer or just use another battery. We'll go with the second option (for our proof of concept). Why? Because a 1S LiPo battery is probably going to be even lighter than a transformer:

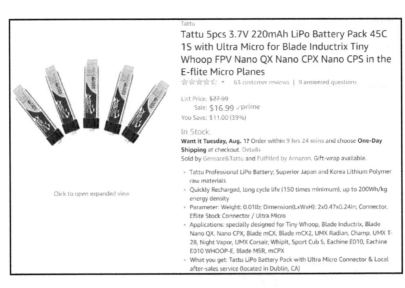

All this logic may seem haphazard to you. But if you look carefully, you'll see how we're constantly balancing weight against cost on every step of the way. We're also attacking the capabilities of our final goals before we even begin to tackle the actual drone itself. There is a definite logic to our madness.

Each of these batteries only weighs about 4.6 grams, and we get five with our purchase. So far, that brings our total weight budget to 584.6 grams, and our money budget to $622.60. We're actually doing pretty well so far. Generally, on a (proof of concept) aerial drone, you'd like to stay less than $3 per gram. So far, we're doing very well.

Finally, we can actually move on to our aerial platform.

The actual aerial platform – drone

Here's the key—don't choose something that you're taking chances with. As for the proof of concept airframe, choose something that has been around for a long time, proven itself over the years, isn't (necessarily) the cheapest thing, but is certainly not the most expensive. To prove your concept, don't get fancy. Just pick something tried and true, and that can definitely lift your payload. Our payload (not including batteries) is 584.6 grams.

The most tried and trued drone platform (aside from a Phantom) is a DJI Flame Wheel. The Flame Wheel F550 is a hexacopter (6 rotors) and has a maximum takeoff weight of 1,200 g-2,400 g. This means our airframe, motors, battery, and ESC can weigh between 615.4 grams and 1815.4 grams. That's a lot of variance, why?

Well, the Flame Wheel F550 is capable of running different props, and 3S (11.1v) or 4S (14.8v) batteries. The motors are rated in KVm (revolutions per volt). So, the more voltage the faster the props will spin, and the more lift it will generate.

Of course, regardless of our weight, we're going to use 4S batteries. It'll give us more leeway in our lift capacity and handling.

The F550 with E300 propulsion system we bought are shown in the following screenshot:

VtooLand

Dji F550 Flame Wheel Arf Kit

☆☆☆☆☆ ▾   10 customer reviews | 14 answered questions

Note: This item is only available from third-party sellers (see all offers).

Available from these sellers.

- Ultrastrength Material Frame Arms adopt PA66+30GF ultrastrength material design, providing better crashworthiness
- Attractive Frame Arms Provide different color frame arms: red, white, black, which makes your flight more colorful.
- Integrated PCB Wiring The use of high strength compound PCB frame board, makes wiring of ESCs and battery safer and easier
- Huge Assembly Space Optimized frame design, which provides abundant assembly space for autopilot systems.

The Flame Wheel airframe, motors, ESCs, and props weigh about 2.9 lbs (1,315.5 grams). That brings our total weight up to 1,897.1 grams (well below our maximum takeoff weight of 2,400 grams). This means we have about 502.9 g to spend on batteries, and Pixhawk.

Batteries

We want 4S batteries. We need the power. Unfortunately, there's a weight problem in that the battery weight is increased by 25% over a 3S. (The *s* is how many cells the battery holds.)

We need to leave 150 g to 200 g for our Pixhawk + accessories (GPS, and so on). So we have 300 g to 350 g to spend on batteries. Unfortunately, that greatly limits our mAh (milliamp hour) rating. Basically, that rating is how many milliamps the battery can expend in one hour.

The bigger the number, the longer your potential flight time. Theoretically, in reality, the more mAh you have, the heavier your battery, and the more that affects your overall flight time. It's the law of diminishing returns. For example, you won't see twice the flight time from a 6,000 mAh battery as you would from a 3,000 mAh battery. It would be more like (not actual just for the purposes of an example) 15% (if you could even get the aircraft off the ground).

We found these batteries right in the sweet spot of 328 g:

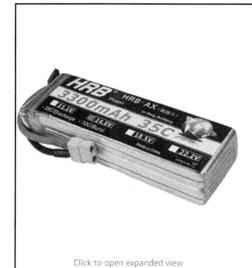

HRB

HRB 4s lipo battery 14.8V 3300mah 35C XT60 Plug For Quadcopter Helicopter RC Car Boat bateria lipo AKKU Trex-450 480

Be the first to review this item

Price: $33.99 & **FREE Shipping**

Note: Not eligible for Amazon Prime.

Only 9 left in stock - order soon.
Get it as soon as Aug. 3 - 8 when you choose **Expedited Shipping** at checkout. Ships from and sold by Yowoohrb.

- HRB Brand Lithium Polymer (LiPo) Battery
- 1 year warranty and friendly customer service.
- Application:RC airplane, helicopter, car, truck, boat, drone, etc.(Only if the voltage, dimension and the plug match, then it will fit).
- Notice: Don't over charge more than 4.2V and dont over discharge below 3.7V

Click to open expanded view

That brings our monetary budget to $622.60 (so far) + $66.98 (two batteries) + $310 (Flame Wheel airframe) for a total of $1,000.58. Really, that's pretty inexpensive for a proof of concept drone.

Now, we need to run some calculations to see if this thing will even fly.

Running the numbers

We're not going to bore you with all of the calculations involved in computing your potential flight times. Instead, there's an extremely handy online calculator for helping you with your multicopter designs at `https://www.ecalc.ch/xcoptercalc.php`.

The results we get with this configuration are shown in the following screenshot:

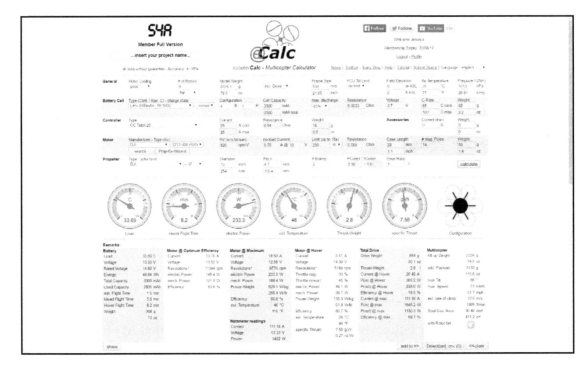

I know the font is really small to read. The bottom line? We get about 5.5 minutes of flight time. If we were going into a production prototype, we'd spend a ton of time (and probably a lot more money) tweaking our parts until we reach just the right balance of flight time and payload. But this is certainly not a production prototype. Not with the camera we'd want to eventually carry, and nowhere near the size we'd eventually want to go for. For a simple proof of concept, we can deal with 5-minute flights. If we really want, we can bump that up to just over 7 minutes with a 5,000 mAh battery. But that may overload our motors if we ever go full throttle. Let's not risk it.

Again, this low flight time may shock you, if you're used to a DJI Phantom, Inspire, and so on. But again, this is not a full production drone. This is just proof of concept. Not of balancing battery to drive to weight, but of flying a 360 camera, and successfully stabilizing it with a custom system.

For those purposes, 5 minutes is not great, but certainly not bad either (especially for our budget). With the right tweaks to our hardware and budget we could easily expect to exceed 20-minute flight times. Again though we're under a time crunch. A cost of $1,000 (not including the Pixhawk) for a fully functional proof of concept, minus the stamina of a production prototype, should be enough to get a Kickstarter campaign going. Or enough to at least prove that we can build such a drone to a potential investor. The rest is just tuning (picking just the right size, hardware, and batteries).

Now, let's build our proof of concept machine.

Assembling the drone

As predicted, our retractable landing gear has not arrived yet. Not only that, they are having issues in customs. Good for us! We thought ahead and bought temporary landing gear; $20.99 well spent!

So, here's a glimpse of what our assembled drone looks like (with temporary landing gear):

Let's take a quick look at the building techniques on a multicopter drone.

Too many freakin' wires!

That thing looks like a mess, doesn't it? It's not. Cable management is the key. You don't want any wires in danger of obstructing (or even breaking) propellers. That spells instant crash. The following image shows how the wires to the ESCs and motors are routed under the airframe and bundled:

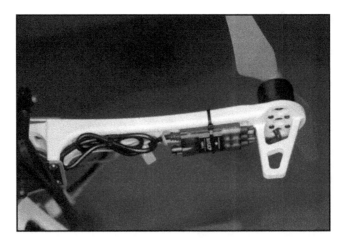

Not only that, but **electromagnetic (EM)** interference is your enemy in the air. It can completely disrupt your video, telemetry, GPS, or even control signals. So never wrap your cables in circles. Instead, notice that they're wrapped up in figure-eights (especially power leads).

Since we're on this angle—don't leave out any screws! A lot of old-school drone pilots come from the fixed-wing world. A common practice in these circles is to only screw down motors with two screws. Don't do that. If a screw vibrates loose, and you lose a motor, your multicopter can turn into a rock falling from the sky pretty quickly.

When dealing with multicopters, you have to remember that even a piano has a better glide profile than a multicopter.

It's not unheard of for kit manufacturers to throw in a few extra screws. If you find extra screws when you are done, double-check every screw to make sure you put them in. If they seem superfluous they're not.

GPS on a stick

You may also notice that the GPS antenna is mounted on a mast (as shown in the following image):

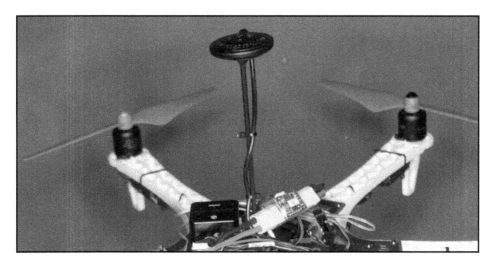

You want your GPS to be well out of the plane of your motors. Remember that electric motors work via a magnetic field. The very definition of EM, right? So keep it up and out of the way of these motors. The plane that the motors are running on won't necessarily kill your GPS. But it could. Why take the chance, right? It may look weird. But a crashed drone looks worse.

Rails are awesome

Rails have been used in the television and film industry for a very long time. Simply put, they're a standardized system for mounting accessories. In fact, rails (in several different forms) are used in everything from firearms (picatinny rails for sights, flashlights, lasers, and other accessories) to cinema cameras (for matte boxes, follow focus, monitors, external hard drives, and so on). Rails for drones are the center of a drone. All major hardware is attached to the rails. The main airframe, the landing gear, the gimbal, and even in most cases, the batteries are mounted to the rails. You can see the rails for our drone in the following image:

Here, you can see the two carbon fiber tubes (the rails) with the airframe attached (using rubber grommets inside of aluminum d-rings), our gimbal attached, the landing gear supports attached, and even a blank rail mount (top) in case we decide to mount another accessory in the future.

You can get an idea of just how useful rails are. It's a pretty simple concept, really. Most accessories simply snap into place on the rail system. Rails are very handy and awesome.

Anything loose? Tuck it away and tie it down

In the following image, you can see that not every servo connection was plugged in. As we had no need to tilt or pan the gimbal during flight (remember, it's a 360 camera), we didn't bother connecting up those controls for the gimbal. But we don't want loose wires flailing about and possibly hitting our rotors. So they're tucked into the frame with just the ends poking out in case we change our mind later on the subject. Also, wherever possible, we tucked wires deeper into the frame, and wherever not; we used zip ties to hold them together. There are no less than five zip ties in the following image. Can you spot them all?

Along those same lines, make sure you don't leave anything to chance with components. Simply strapping down batteries isn't enough. Velcro them to make sure they don't slip free; 3M automotive tape is also great for fixing things down in a more permanent way. The following image shows the battery for the FPV camera, as well as the camera itself. Notice that the camera is fixed with a piece of grey 3M automotive tape, and the battery is fixed using Velcro (currently placed on its side to show the Velcro).

Automotive tape, Velcro, and zip ties are your best friends with multicopter building.

Hooking up the ESCs to Pixhawk

Pixhawk can handle all sorts of multicopters. The following chart illustrates the types of multicopters as well as their motor numbers:

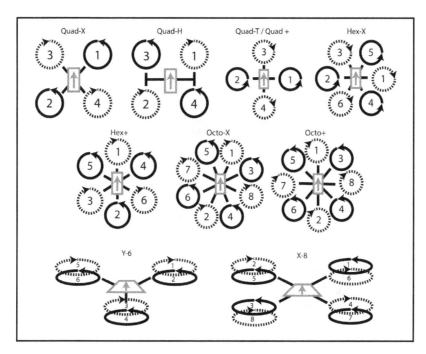

As you can see, there are a lot of different types of multicopters, so don't let yourself fall into my personal pet peeve—someone who calls them all quads. They're certainly not all quads. The direction of the circles in the graphic illustrate the direction that the motors/propellers must turn in order for the multicopters to fly properly with Pixhawk. The numbers correspond to the `Main Out` number on the servo board of the Pixhawk.

The following image shows our six servo wires (as this drone is a Hex-X configuration) plugged into their proper ports on Pixhawk:

To check the motor-spin directions (and make sure they're accurate), you'll have to power everything on. But you won't be able to do that until you configure the Pixhawk.

Before applying any power to your drone, you must take off the propellers!

Configuring Pixhawk and Mission Planner

We're going to set this up in several very cool ways. Here are our goals:

1. Get the basic configuration of Pixhawk installed for multicopter operation.
2. Hook up our FPV camera so that we receive the signal on the ground, and put it up in the Mission Planner interface. This way, we can watch one screen to get all our information.

3. Set up a set of joysticks so that we can fly the multicopter with traditional helicopter-style (real-world) controls.

So, without further delay let's get started on this!

The initial configuration of Pixhawk

Obviously, plug in your Pixhawk to your computer via USB, connect to it in Mission Planner, and start up the wizard. First, let's run through the multirotor version of the setup wizard, and then we'll tweak things:

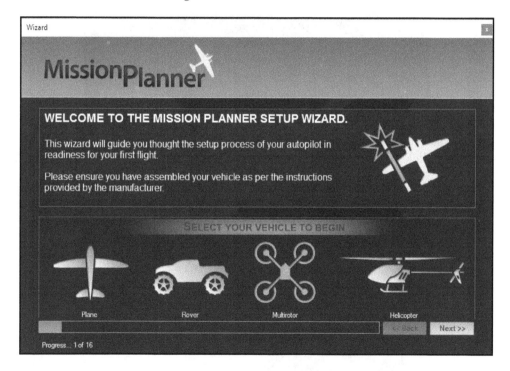

We're going to walk through each screen. By now, a lot of this will just be old hat. But still, information is better said and not needed than needed and not said.

Of course, select **Multirotor** as our vehicle type. Then, you'll be confronted with this screen to narrow down the multitude of multirotor types:

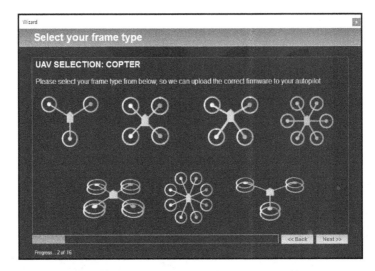

Obviously, we select the hexacopter from the list. But here's where things get a bit confusing. After clicking on **Next**, we're confronted with a bunch of quads and a Y6. What the what?

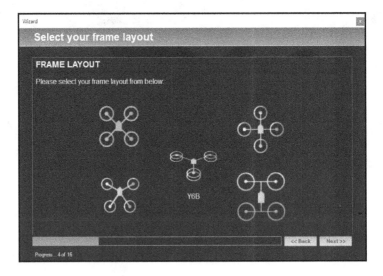

This is (admittedly) confusing. But really, what the software is trying to ascertain is whether your hexacopter is a Hex-X or Hex+ type frame. I (personally) have never seen a Hex-H frame, nor a Hex frame that is spread in the front. But maybe they exist somewhere. So, even though it shows only four rotors, we choose the x-frame. In the previous screen, we selected a Hexacopter, then we chose the x-frame variety. This makes it a Hex-X.

During the next section, we'll calibrate the accelerometers so that the Pixhawk knows when the aircraft is level versus tilted:

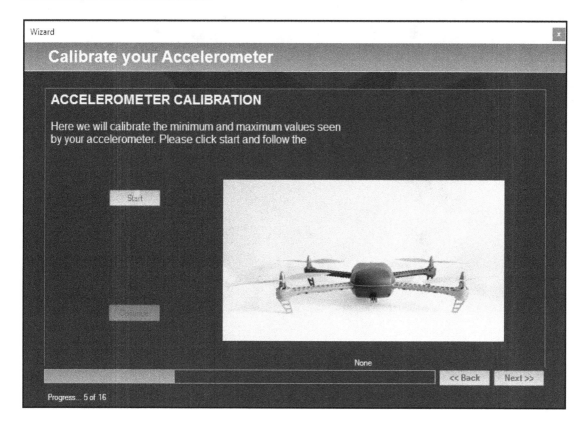

Instead of just clicking on **Next**, this time you'll want to click on **Start**. Upon starting calibration, the software will ask you to set the aircraft level, then tilt it 90° on the left, 90° on the right, on the nose, the tail, then upside down.

The next step is compass calibration. For this one, you'll want to be very mindful of the USB cable.

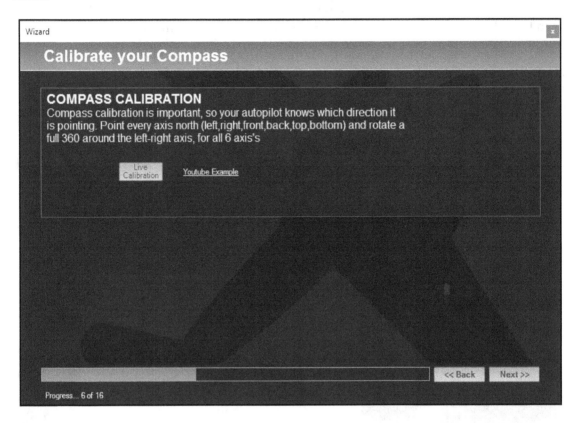

Once you click on **Live Calibration**, you're going to be asked to rotate the drone on every axis a full 360°. You'll be confronted with another interface that shows the data points of your rotation. Once you've hit every white dot, the interface will automatically close. Do not click on the **Done** button. This will register as an uncalibrated compass. Just keep rotating your drone in all directions until the interface closes itself.

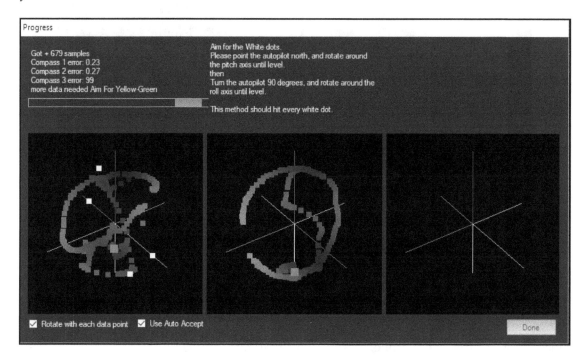

Let's skip over binding the radio, and selecting our power module. We've covered that section pretty well in our other chapters. If you need any help, just refer back to these chapters. For now, let's set up our flight modes:

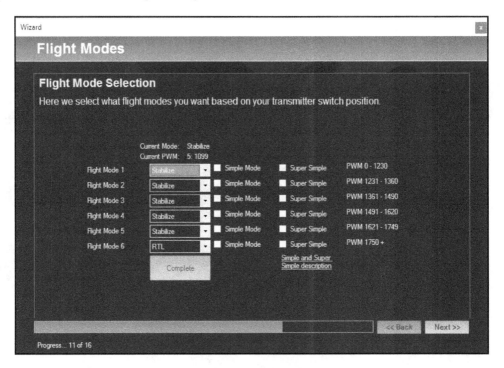

Since this is our first aerial drone, let's go over flight modes quickly:

- **Stabilize**: The standard flight mode, which uses all the available sensors to fly in the most stabile fashion possible. Think of this mode as analogous to DJI's ATTI mode.

- **Altitude Hold (Alt Hold)**: When this mode is engaged, the drone will maintain its current altitude while you can concentrate on the position and orientation of the aircraft. If using the standard Pixhawk hardware, a barometer is used to maintain the altitude; this means it is **above sea level** (**ASL**). If there are changing barometric pressures, this can affect the actual altitude that is held. However, if a downward-facing range finder (as we used for collision avoidance with our golf trolley) is used, the Pixhawk will use this as a primary sensor for **above ground level** (**AGL**) altitude hold (within the limits of the sensor's range). Therefore, I advise you fit a LIDAR sensor if you plan to use this mode.

- **Loiter**: This is similar to the stabilize mode. A pilot may still fly the multicopter as if in a manual mode, but when the sticks are released the drone will slow to a stop and maintain altitude, attitude, and position. You should only use this mode in an environment with low EM, and have a very good calibration on your sensors.

- **Return to Launch (RTL)**: When RTL mode is engaged, the drone will attempt to fly back to its original launch point and land. The `RTL_ALT` parameter is used as the AGL altitude for this maneuver. The drone will first rise to the `RTL_ALT` (in meters, and the default is 15), fly (in a straight line) back to the launch point, and then execute a landing (straight down from hover).

- **Auto**: When engaged, this will trigger autopilot. It will execute a preprogrammed set of waypoints (GPS coordinates that indicate a target location), can hover at these waypoints for a specified period of time, and execute do commands (such as click off a camera shutter, drop a payload—such as a bottle of water to someone awaiting rescue, or just about anything else that Pixhawk can control), and then move on to the next waypoint. This mode is used quite often in mapping, surveying, or inspecting.

- **Acro**: This mode is commonly used for racing drones. Acro stands for Acrobatic. No stabilization is given. When you input via the sticks, the drone will do whatever you tell it (including crash). You can execute flips, tricks, rolls, and so on. It's not advisable for a payload drone (such as the one we just built). Consider this the no limits mode.

- **AutoTune**: It's extremely handy if you're building your own drone. This mode runs through a 5-7 minute tuning cycle. Basically, what it does is run through a series of twitches to set the rates on the stabilization and controls to match a 90° per second attitude rate on axis, and reduces the stabilization rates so that when the drone reaches a state of equilibrium, it doesn't bounce back, but stops rotating dead still. You must make sure to execute this mode in a very wide open area, as the drone will drift greatly during this procedure. If you need to correct the drone's position, the mode will be temporarily suspended (until the sticks are returned to the middle position). Take off in **Stabilize**, or **Alt Hold**, and then engage **AutoTune** while in the air.

- **Brake**: This attempts to stop the drone as quickly as possible when the sticks are returned to middle position.

- **Circle**: This mode should really be called orbit. Circling implies that the drone flies in a circle around a target with the nose pointed toward the direction of the flight. This is of course true with airplanes (which we'll get into in the next chapter). However, with multicopters, this mode keeps the nose pointed at a target. It can be extremely useful for cinematic shots, as well as for security systems and surveillance. Setting the CIRCLE_RADIUS parameter to 0 will keep the drone in one spot and rotate the drone on the yaw axis until disengaged. This can be useful for panorama shots. When engaged, the pilot has no control over the roll and pitch of the aircraft, but can change its altitude.

- **Drift**: It's a great mode for beginners or fixed wing pilots. If you're familiar with fixed wing controls, this is rather like a bank and yank setup. The Pixhawk controls the yaw and roll automatically. The left stick is only used to control altitude (throttle), and the right stick controls pitch. Moving the right stick left or right will execute an automatic turn (normally a combination of yaw and roll) with the user only needing to input (via that x-axis on the right stick) the rate of that turn.

- **Guided/Guided_NoGPS**: This mode is not traditionally activated using a standard radio. You would want to activate this mode using a GCS (ground control station) such as a laptop. It lets you click on various points on the map, and the drone will automatically fly to this waypoint. Think of it like an interactive Auto mode.

- **Land**: This will attempt to automatically bring the drone down and land it. Upon landing, it will automatically shut off the motors and disarm the drone. Personally, I wouldn't advise using this mode unless you have a downward facing rangefinder LIDAR.

- **PosHold**: Rather like loiter, whenever the sticks are returned to the center position, PosHold will attempt to hold the drone in one place. Consider this the mirror to a DJI Phantom's standard GPS mode.

- **Sport**: This is a bit misleading. This is not the mode for racing drones. Rather, this was meant for the film industry to be able to fly high-speed dolly style shots low to the ground. It's a combination of **Stabilize** and Altitude Hold (**Alt Hold**). It will hold the altitude where the left stick (throttle) is +/- 10% of middle (using a downward-facing rangefinder, optimally). The vehicle will not lean more than 45° on the tilt/roll axis, and it will maintain that angle until brought back (no position hold). The pilot can still climb or descend at up to 2.5 m/s if outside of that +/- 10% of mid-position on throttle.

- **Throw**: Personally, I'm never inclined to even try this mode. It allows the user to throw the drone into the air in order to start the motors (for instance, if you want to fly a drone off a small boat, but don't want to risk hitting a railing on takeoff). It's not just dangerous for the drone, it's also dangerous for the user. If the drone isn't thrown far enough away before the motors start spinning up, it could come back at you and slice you up while it's trying to stabilize itself. Then the question needs to be asked, "If I needed this to launch it, where am I supposed to land it?" This mode is pretty useless (and dangerous) in my opinion.

- **Follow Me**: This is the same mode we used for the golf trolley. First, using a Bluetooth module to fly your drone isn't all that advisable (due to the limited range), and who wants to walk around with a laptop? And then there are things such as trees and hung wires. Follow Me has been around on drones for quite a while. I still have yet to see footage shot in this mode that was equal to that shot using a pilot at the sticks. And I've seen far too many crashes to make this mode worth using on a multicopter. I don't advise it. But hey, it's your drone and investment.

- **Simple/Super Simple**: Again, I find these misleading. **Simple** and **Super Simple** modes keep the drone's controls in relation to its heading at takeoff (**Simple**) or arming (**Super Simple**). So, if you turn the aircraft 90° to the left after takeoff, and push the pitch stick forward it will actually tilt to the right and move in the direction (that would have been) forward at takeoff. It's helpful for pilots that tend to lose orientation of the aircraft when it's in the air. Pilots used to flying though tend to get confused by this mode (why I find it misleading), and find it very frustrating.

- **ADS-B Ping**: **Automatic Dependent Surveillance Broadcast** (**ADS-B**) is the system used by air traffic control to track aircrafts in the air. This system (when implemented into Pixhawk) can allow the drone to avoid near misses automatically. You need to have a uAvionix ADS-B Ping sensor (not carried on the aircraft, but MAVLink enabled) and a ground station. This system would be mostly used for military or commercial drones (big and expenisve ones) that fly at altitudes and areas of controlled air space. It's probably beyond the scope of this book.

Since we have our flight modes on a two-position switch on our standard RC controller, we'll set the base (flight mode 1) to **PosHold**, and our flipped switch (flight mode 6) to RTL. What about the rest? PWM (you can see it on the right of the previous picture) represents the value sent over from the remote controller to the Pixhawk.

A two-position switch would be a PWM < 1230 (off) and a PWM >1750 (on). With more positions on the switch, the number would fall somewhere in between. If the remote is paired and powered on while you're on this screen, as you flip through the positions of the switch, the drop-down menu will highlight green. Just set the desired mode for each position. Make sure you click on **Complete** before clicking on **Next**.

We've been through calibration before. We're only showing this screen at this point to emphasize that you should not forget to reverse any channels that are moving in the wrong direction on your transmitter:

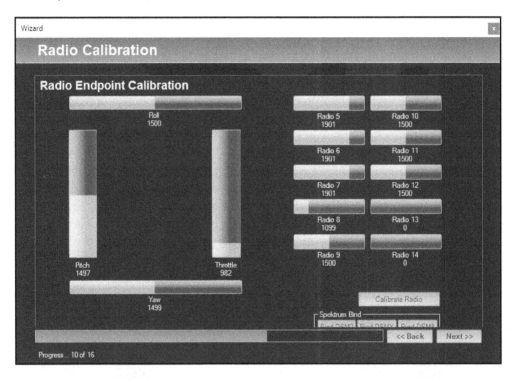

Next, we need to tell Pixhawk how to handle emergencies.

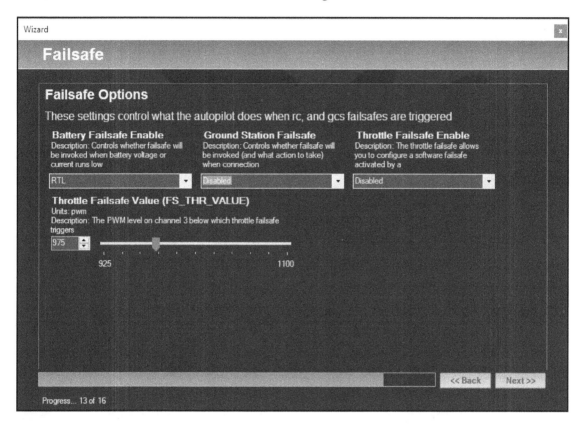

Failsafes are engaged during (what most would call) emergency situations. They can range from engaging a different autonomous flight mode to preventing a user error. Let's take a look at these:

- **Battery Failsafe Enable**: This sets the flight mode to engage if the battery's capacity drops below safe levels.
- **Ground Station Failsafe**: This sets the flight mode if the connection is lost with the ground station. As we're using a ground station (heavily), and don't plan on long-range autonomous flight, we'll set this mode to RTL.
- **Throttle Failsafe Enable**: This sets whether or not the pilot can drop below a specified (using the slider) level during flight. We would neither want to turn off our motors and tumble out of control, nor fly through our own propwash during descent (potentially resulting in a crash).

Geo fencing is another feature you can enable in the setup wizard:

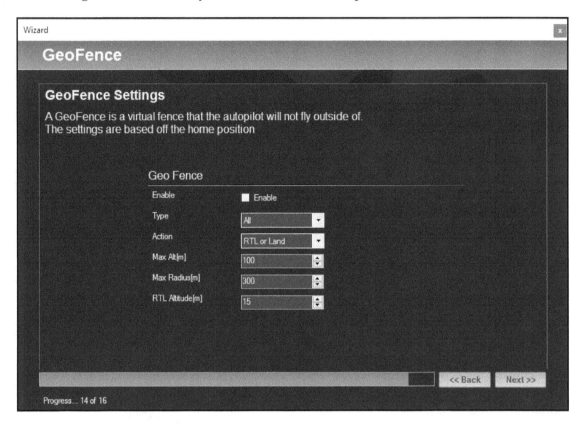

Geo fencing allows you to limit the range and altitude of your drone. The actual limits are pretty self-explanatory, so let's move on.

Configuring the ground station

Here is where we configure our ground station to receive video, use joysticks, and just be all around awesome! Let's start with the joysticks.

Using joysticks to control a drone

TV shows and movies repeatedly show a particular set of (really cool looking) joysticks for controlling drones.

It just so happens that we have a set of these sticks lying around our shop. They're great for flight simulator games. It's not often that the items that movies show as tools are actually as high quality as they look. These things have a ton of buttons (to activate a lot of modes), have a great feel, and are very accurate.

They're Saitek X52 gaming flight control sticks. And if you'd like to pick up a set, here they are on Amazon:

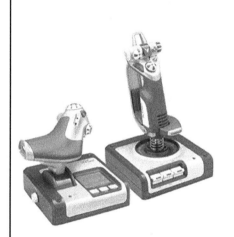

Logitech

Logitech G Saitek X52 Flight Control System

☆☆☆☆☆ ▾   51 customer reviews | 15 answered questions

Price: $149.99 ✓prime

In Stock.
Want it Thursday, Aug. 3? Order within 18 hrs 3 mins and choose **One-Day Shipping** at checkout. Details
Ships from and sold by Amazon.com. Gift-wrap available.

- Advanced Multi-Function Display (MFD) for real flying interaction
- 2 dedicated MFD buttons and 2 rotary dials with in-built buttons to control additional game functionality
- Joystick with precision centering mechanism, non-contact technology on X and Y axes and constant spring force
- Progressive throttle with tension adjustment, detents for afterburner and idle; 2 fire buttons
- Works with: Windows XP, XP64 and Vista (all versions) and Windows 7, Windows 8.1, Windows 10 or newer

Roll over image to zoom in

We're going to use a Windows laptop for our ground station. When setting up Mission Planner's joystick functionality, it's a good idea to have the properties window for your game controller open. It will show what button is being pushed by highlighting it. Although we probably won't need it, it's still a good idea to have it open on the side. For the Saitek sticks, it looks similar to the following screenshot:

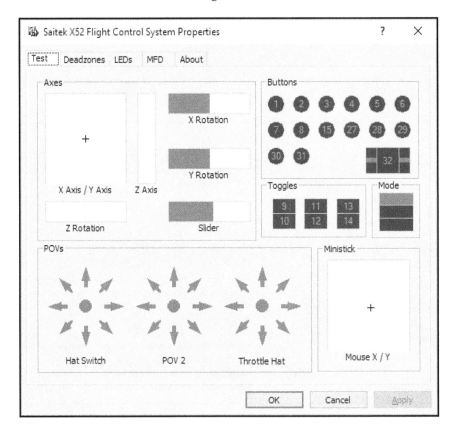

As you can see there are lots of buttons. There's even a Thinkpad style button mouse that you could potentially use to control a gimbal (if we were interested in doing that).

In Mission Planner, we'll go into the **Config/Tuning** section and select the **Planner** button from the left side. We'll see the following screen:

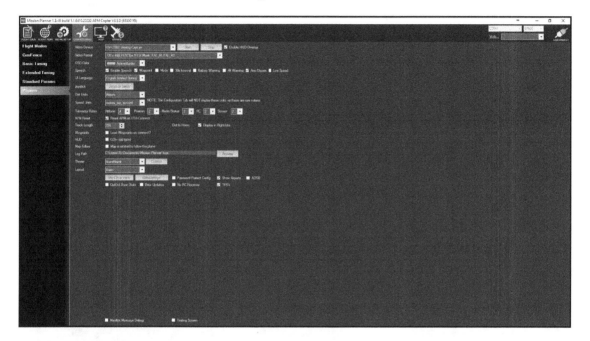

From there, just click on the **Joystick Setup** button. Mission Planner is great. It lets you configure just about anything you need for Pixhawk without having to program anything. Of course the option is open to you if you like. But if you're just starting out it's a great interface. Once the **Joystick** setup window opens, you'll see this:

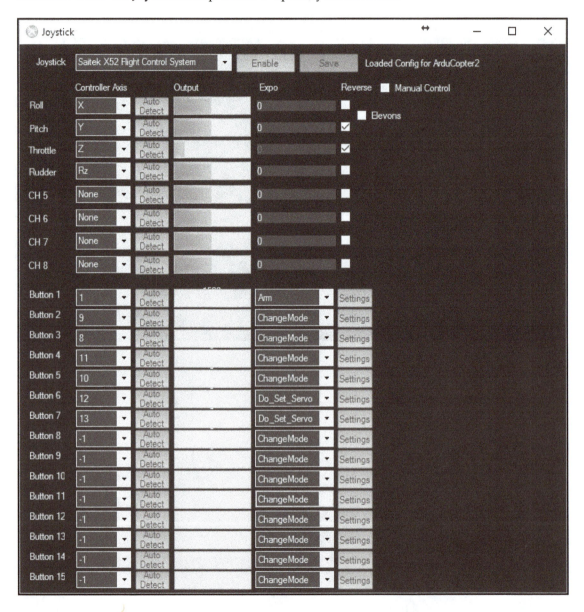

Here is where we can set what every button, stick, dial, and slider on our physical joystick will control.

Once every axis is set on our main controls for **Roll**, **Pitch**, **Throttle**, and **Rudder**, you'll need to make sure that they control the green bars in the correct direction. If they don't, just tick the checkbox in the **Reverse** column.

Setting an axis or button is relatively easy. Just click on the **Auto Detect** button, and an alert will pop up telling you to click on **OK**. Don't move the joystick until you do. Once you click on **OK**, the software will begin listening for movement on the game controls. As soon as you move an axis or press a button, it will register that as the desired control.

You may notice that several buttons have a -1 selected in their **Control Axis** dropdowns. This is a designation which means that the button is unassigned. As with the axis, the **Auto Detect** buttons can automatically assign the physical joystick button to that control.

The next dropdown is the type of control that button is assigned to. You may notice that several are set to **Change Mode**. That's because they set the drone into various flight modes. You can set the flight mode using the **Settings** button next to the dropdown. It will open another window, with yet another dropdown in it.

Similarly, you'll find the Do_Set_Servo type very useful. It can do all sorts of things, from setting servo-plug controlled gimbal modes, to controlling camera functions via a servo-plug, to raising and lowering retractable landing gear. Basically, it can set a servo value for just about anything controlled via servo-plug. All you have to do is open the **Settings** dialog, and select the output port on Pixhawk, then tell it what you want that PWM value of the control to be (remember, the PWM value we were talking about when we set up flight modes on the controller). You're just mimicking what you'd like it to be as if you flipped a switch on a standard RC remote. On our two Do_Set_Servo functions, we're using a toggle switch on the joystick. One direction sets the PWM to 0 (lowered landing gear), and the other direction sets the PWM to 1,800 (raised landing gear).

Once you've finished configuring a joystick, all you really have to do is click on **Save** at the top of the interface, and then click on **Enable** before closing the window.

If everything is working properly, you'll see the following in the upper-left of the map window:

Setting up video

There are essentially two components to getting the video up on the laptop screen:

1. Receive the transmission.
2. Digitize it into the laptop.

We chose our Spektrum FPV camera and transmitter because it was inexpensive and light. But we also chose it because it uses the most common set of frequencies in FPV: Fatshark. So, finding a Fatshark receiver for our ground station will be easy and also inexpensive. Here's the one we arrived at:

The listing says that it's currently unavailable but I'm sure it will be back in stock soon. It was when I bought it just a couple weeks ago. We paid only $35 US for it. And we're sure that even if it's not in stock, you could find something similar with no issues. You can't spit on FPV without hitting something Fatshark.

Now, we just need something inexpensive to convert the analog video signal to USB so Mission Planner can read it. And here we go:

Now, it's just a matter of going back to Mission Planner's config/tuning and planner screen. It's fairly self-explanatory just select the video device, and set up the options as shown in the following screenshot:

What this does is it swaps out the artificial horizon on the upper left of our flight interface with the FPV view and **on-screen display** (**OSD**) telemetry overlaid on it as shown in the following screenshot:

And there we have it! We're ready to do our test flights, right? Wrong. If you remember, during the assembly stage we needed to put off part of that until we could spin up our motors. We're at that stage. If you notice from the FPV camera there are no propellers on the drone. Never even think about attempting the next stage unless you've removed the propeller first.

Final configuration before test flights

Before trying to fly this thing, we need to make sure that every motor is hooked up to the right spot and is turning in the right direction. Remember our chart from before? Here's just the Hex-X from it as well as the Pixhawk with the six-motor servo ports highlighted:

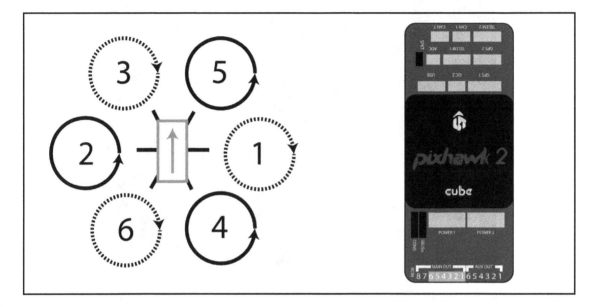

Back in Mission Planner (while connected to your powered-on drone), go into **Initial Setup**, and under the **Option Hardware** section you'll find **Motor Test**. It looks like the following screenshot:

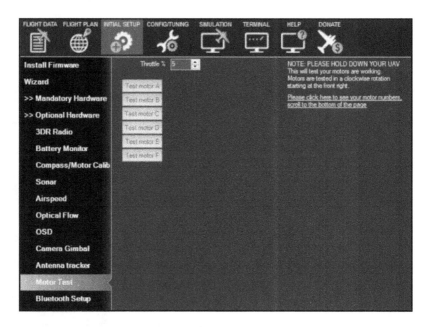

And here's the weird part. This test does not test the motors in number sequence. Not the same numbers as in the graph on the previous page. That number sequence only represents which motors are plugged into which port. Instead, these motor test buttons start with motor number 5, and then go in sequence around the aircraft in a clockwise fashion. This means they go in this order for a Hex-X:

- Button A = Motor #5
- Button B = Motor #1
- Button C = Motor #4
- Button D = Motor #6
- Button E = Motor #2
- Button F = Motor #3

I know, it's not consistent. But think about it this way—the person building the drone is often not the person flying the drone. Making the motor test in an easy sequence is one way of making sure a user won't get confused. Honestly, I'm not sure why they didn't just put the motors in sequence in the same way on the servo board. I'm sure there's some reason though.

If the motors don't power on as shown earlier, but come on in the wrong order that means that you've hooked things up on the servo board a bit wonky, and will have to switch up some servo cables to the right ports. If the motors spin in the wrong direction (refer to the graph that indicates the spin direction), all you have to do is unplug two of the three leads going from the ESC on that motor, and swap them. It doesn't matter which two.

And now that this test is over with we're finally ready to do some flights!

When you test, start off small. Just do some hover tests using the standard RC controller. If something isn't to your liking, only change one thing at a time. If something goes wrong that will at least tell you how. Too many changes between flights mean too many variables to troubleshoot.

And here's what our final setup looks like:

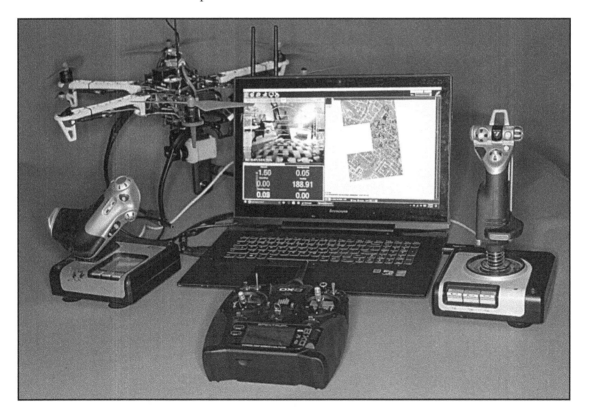

Summary

In this chapter, we learned a bit more on the philosophy of prototyping, kitbashing, and altering prefab parts for our purposes. We also learned how to configure Pixhawk for a multicopter, include a video feed in our laptop display, and use joysticks to control a drone. If that wasn't enough, we also learned how to balance power to weight on a multicopter. Now, you can see just what complicated beasts they are.

In the next chapter, we're going to take on the Holy Grail of dronery: a fixed wing drone. In a lot of ways, they're simpler than multicopters. But in reality they're not.

7

The Holy Grail - A Fixed Wing Drone

Wow for a holy grail, she sure is one ugly pig, right? Well, prototypes just aren't usually pretty. So, why is a fixed wing drone (like the airplane in the following image) considered a holy grail?

The answer is pretty simple, actually. Airplanes need to keep moving in order to stay airborne. Go too slow, and you stall (a fancy word for fall from the sky until you build up speed again except that it's usually vertical speed, and vertical speed is going down).

With multicopters, tuning them is fairly easy: take it off, hover just **outside of ground effect (OGE)**, and let it *twitch* around a bit. If it's too crazy, just land it, reset the settings, and repeat. Since an airplane is constantly moving tuning can be quite a bit more hazardous to the aircraft.

While tuning fixed wings, I've had them turn into lawn darts, porpoise like dolphins jumping out of the ocean, and (as stated in a previous chapter) blow their wings right off. So, it's important while prototyping to start with an airframe that is relatively inexpensive yet stable. It's also important to choose one that offers some protection for your Pixhawk if something does go wrong. That makes a foamie airplane a perfect choice. Foam airplanes are very cheap, and are basically flying packing material. It's certainly no guarantee that the Pixhawk would survive a crash. But it does improve its chances.

The following topics will be covered in this chapter:

- Why this particular airplane kit?
- The assembly
- Tuning a fixed wing aircraft with mission planner
- Setting up for tuning
- The tuning process
- Autotune flight

Why this particular airplane kit?

The plane we're using (as shown in the following image) is a Bixler from Hobby King. It's actually named after one of the two Joshes (Josh Bixler) from the popular YouTube channel *Flite Test*:

As you can see, it's very inexpensive. Well under $100, and comes with a motor, and all the servos necessary to fly it. The dihedral curve in the wing makes it uniquely stable for soaring. It also comes with the two halves of the main fuselage separated (making wire routing and component placement very easy). Finally, it's a powered glider. This means it's very efficient, and has the potential to travel great distances under minimal power. This is exactly what we're looking for!

The assembly

Before we get into the parts and specific placement thereof, let's take a quick look at the sketch for this drone:

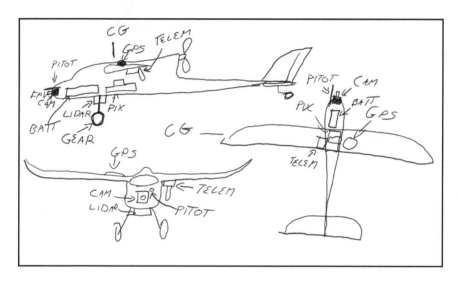

I know but what can I say? I like to sketch out my ideas over a bottle of wine.

The peripherals we're using are the same as all our other drones, with the addition of a pitot tube. We talked about pitot tubes before, but as a quick refresher, a pitot tube is simply a device that measures the air-speed of your aircraft. Think about it—speed is relative. Believe it or not, even when you're standing still, you're traveling at 113,000 mph. Yes, that's right... why? Because the Earth rotates at 1,000 mph + the Earth around the sun is 67,000 mph, plus the solar system's speed through the universe is 45,000 mph. But on Earth, your speed is 0 mph because your speed is measured relative to the ground (Earth).

So when flying, you have two speeds—your ground speed (your speed relative to the Earth), and your air speed (your speed through the air). Think about it. If you're traveling into the wind at a 60 mph airspeed, and that wind is 10 mph, your ground speed is 50 mph (60-10=50). GPS measures your ground speed. But in order to keep from stalling, you need a device that measures your air speed. Enter the pitot tube (as shown in the following image, the silver tube extends from the front of the aircraft to the right of our FPV camera):

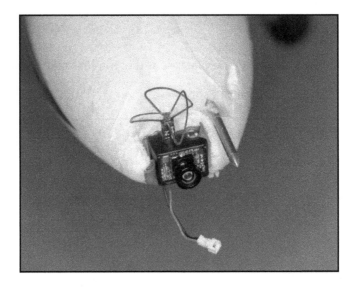

There are digital and analog pitot tubes. I recommend using the digital PX4 pitot tube. It's far easier to implement (via I2C), and really isn't that expensive. Here's the one we picked up for our airplane:

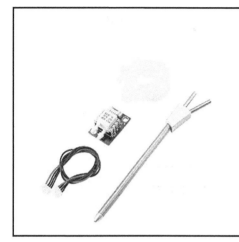

Hobby Signal

Pixhawk PX4 Air Speedometer Airspeed Sensor Gauge with Differential Pitot Tube Airspeed Meter/ Gauge Tube 4525DO

Be the first to review this item

Price: $68.99 ✓prime

Only 14 left in stock - order soon.
Want it Thursday, Aug. 24? Order within 13 hrs 50 mins and choose **One-Day Shipping** at checkout. Details
Sold by Hobby Signal and Fulfilled by Amazon. Gift-wrap available.

- The modified version of airspeed tube adopts 4525do digital differential pressure sensor, i2c communication, suitable for pixhawk px4 original firmware.
- Different from analog differential pressure sensor for apm, it can be used with apm.
- Package includes: 1 x airspeed module, 1 x pitot tube, 1 x silicone tube, 1 x 4 pin cable.

New (2) from $68.99 ✓prime

Report incorrect product information.

The first thing you may say is, "wait... there's only one I2C port, but now you're using your LIDAR (I2C), and a pitot tube (also I2C) whaaaaaat?" Again, I2C, USB, CAN, and so on these are all digital protocols for information across multiple peripherals and are all capable of using hubs. One of the (many) reasons we lean toward I2C with Pixhawk 2.1 is because it comes with an I2C hub. Just like with a USB hub on your computer; just plug the I2C hub into your Pixhawk's I2C port, and all other I2C peripherals into the hub.

Assembling an airplane is a pretty straightforward process. And the airplane itself (whatever airframe you go with) will come with instructions. So, we're not going to bore you with that stuff. Let's get into the placement of the Pixhawk components.

Placing the Pixhawk

You can't just throw your Pixhawk anywhere inside (or on top of) your plane. Why? Because (believe it or not), you don't want the plane rotating on its axis, and the Pixhawk thinking something else is going on. "Huh?" you're probably asking. Your Pixhawk needs to be located as close to (if not directly on) the **center of gravity** (**CG**) as possible. In an airplane, this is generally at the peak of the top-curve of the main wing. Of course, if it's a faster plane (with swept wings), the CG may be further back and you should refer to the airplane's build instructions.

The following image shows how the Pixhawk's sensors may be affected by placing it away from the CG:

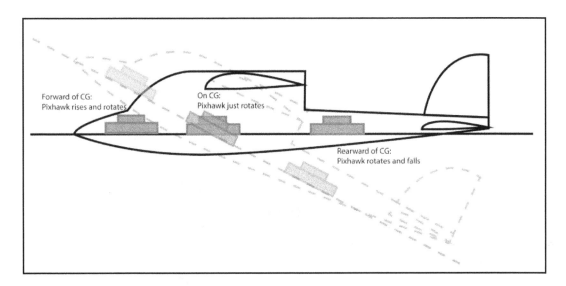

So, the last thing you want is Pixhawk thinking it's doing something that it's not. When the plane noses up (as in this example), and isn't actually rising (for instance, in a landing), if the Pixhawk believes that the plane is rising, it may cut power, or dip the nose back down. Ideally, you want Pixhawk knowing exactly what the plane is doing and doing as little guess work as possible.

Placing the components

As we've said many times, it's important to keep the GPS receiver well away from any **Electromagnetic interference** (**EMI**). So, you'll want to keep it away from transmitters (such as telemetry and **first-person view** (**FPV**)) and motors.

And that's why our sketch was important. We want the GPS fairly close to the CG but we want to avoid that rearward-facing motor right at the back of the wing. We can't place it in the nose because that's where the video transmitter will be. So, by erasing and redrawing, we can find the right place, which is on the top-side of the right wing, close to the fuselage (as shown in the following image):

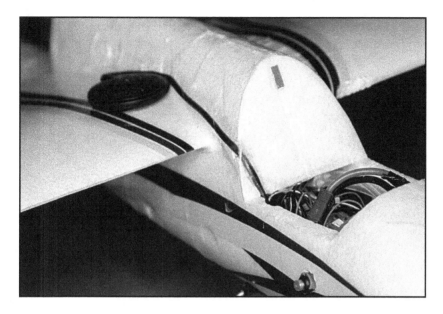

With the canopy off the airplane, you can also see that the cable for the GPS receiver runs through a channel in the foam behind the canopy (so it can fit on snugly). One of the beauties of working with foam is that a soldering iron (set on high) will melt and vaporize foam. So, you can cut through foam extremely easily using just a soldering iron.

You can also see another difficulty with airplanes cables. For aerodynamic reasons (reducing drag), you can't just bundle your cables and zip-tie them to the outside of an airplane (as you could with a multicopter). This makes routing and bundling something that needs to be done with care and planning.

Finally, just under (and forward of) the canopy, you can see the arming switch for the Pixhawk. We drilled a hole (with a soldering iron), and placed the switch in the hole (with some 3M automotive tape). Now, we can arm the airplane without having to do so with the canopy off.

Next is the telemetry transmitter/receiver. Just like with the multicopter, we're going to pilot this drone using joysticks on a laptop. So we need the antenna to be vertical, and out where it can receive (unobstructed). Seems like the underside of the left wing is a great spot (as shown in the following image):

You'll also notice that we cut a hole in the side of the airframe for access to the USB plug on the side of Pixhawk, and another hole to route the wires for the telemetry radio.

The LIDAR module is going to seriously help us with landings. Pixhawk (when properly set up) can use a rangefinder during landings to land itself (autonomously), including flaring at the end to touch down nice and soft. On a plane, LIDAR is not used for collision avoidance. It's used as an altimeter. For that reason, the best place for it is right between the main landing gear (as shown in the following image):

Finally, it's just a matter of placing the FPV camera. You'll notice we cut a notch in the nose of the airplane (as shown in the following image) using a soldering iron, and used 3M automotive tape to fix it into place. The battery for the camera will just Velcro to the underside of the nose of the plane:

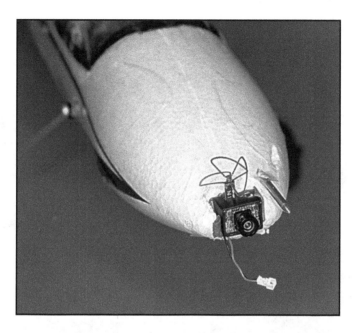

Ok, so now that all of our Pixhawk components are installed (and we've given our fixed wing drone a brain), let's make it smarter through the mission planner settings.

Tuning a fixed wing aircraft with mission planner

By now, you're an expert at installing the right firmware and running through the initial set up within mission planner. So, we're not going to waste your time with all that nonsense at this point. Let's start with setting up the pitot tube.

Configuring the pitot tube

The first thing we have to do is tell Pixhawk to actually use the pitot tube, as well as what kind it is. The following screenshot shows the menu in mission planner, where you will activate the pitot tube we installed:

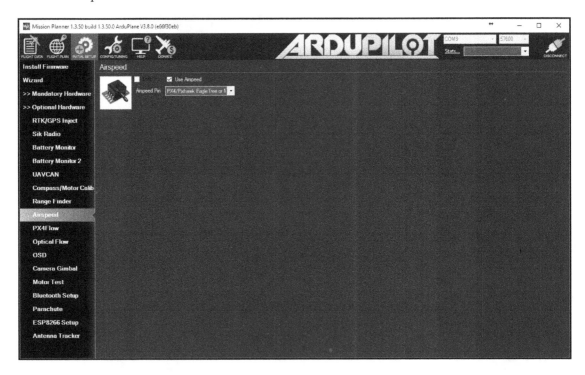

Realizing that it has already been stated, we wish to underscore the need for a pitot tube. Some builders claim that pitot tubes are not required for fixed wing aircraft. Although from a software/hardware standpoint, this is true; in reality, this philosophy couldn't be any more wrong. Using GPS alone only measures ground speed. Without measuring the actual airspeed of the aircraft, going downwind can result in stalls, and going into the wind could result in over-taxing the motors, ESC, or even the airframe.

Remember, that the airplane's lift is strictly determined by achieving a minimum airspeed. Although you may be traveling at 20 mph across the Earth; if you are moving with an 18 mph wind, your airspeed is only 2 mph. Not enough to keep most (if not all) airplanes in the air. Conversely, if you're going into the wind at 20 mph ground speed, your airspeed is now 38 mph. Executing a tight-turn at that airspeed could potentially overtax your wing load and literally blow the wings right off the aircraft.

Therefore, not implementing a pitot tube on a fixed wing aircraft is not only inadvisable it is unsafe, and downright foolish.

And as you can see, the installation and activation of a pitot tube is extremely simple.

To test it, go to the Flight Data screen in Mission Planner and simply blow at the pitot tube. You should see the airspeed go up as shown in the following screenshot:

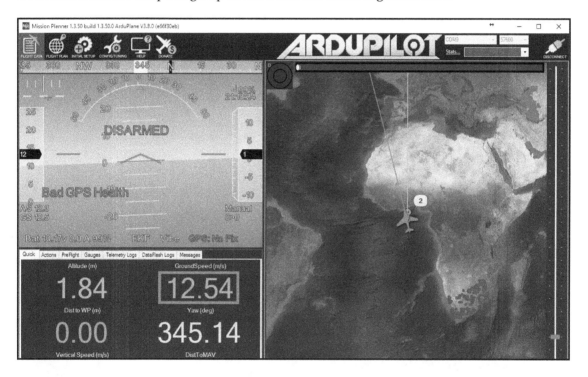

Of course, it does read in the "ground speed" area (the mission planner team never did create a discrete ground speed and air speed readout). But this is, in fact, air speed.

Setting up the LIDAR range finder

Again, this is a piece of hardware that some builders will tell you that you don't need. However, if you plan to autoland your plane you do. GPS and barometric pressure are accurate enough for flight. But they can be off by as much as a meter or more. When your plane is close to the ground, you want Pixhawk to know it. So you need the most accurate altimeter you can get: a rangefinder pointed at the ground:

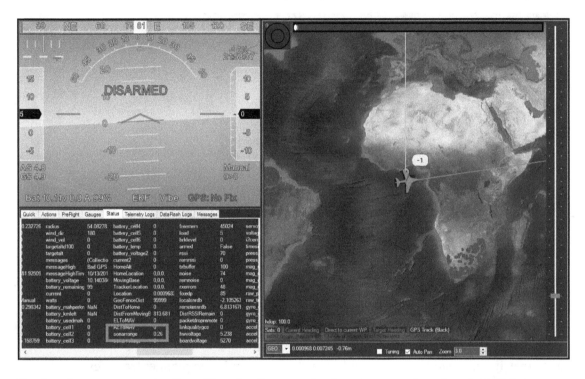

During the setup process (installing the firmware), of course you already selected the TeraRanger rangefinder that we installed. So Pixhawk already knows that the rangefinder is attached. But how does it know when the landing gear have touched down? We have to tell Pixhawk what that height is.

The first step is to get the reading when the aircraft is sitting on the ground. The following screenshot shows where you'll find this (in the **Setup** tab of the Flight Data screen). The current reading is 0.26 (or 26 centimeters).

In the following screenshot, you can see where to set the height of the rangefinder (`RNGFND_GNDCLEAR`) and where to enable the rangefinder function for landing (`RNGFND_LANDING`):

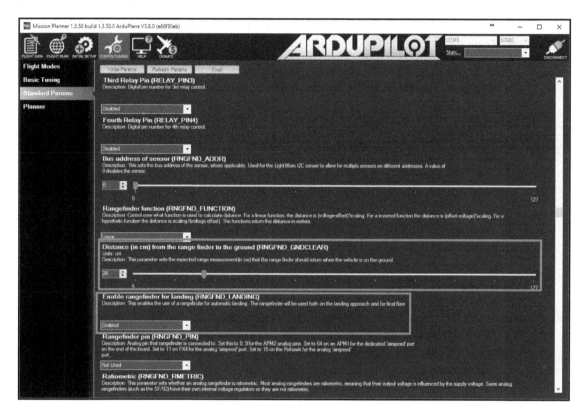

And there it is, all of our specialized sensors are set up. Let's take a quick look at some special considerations before we get into the actual testing procedures to tune our aircraft.

Setting up for tuning

Much like the multirotor version of Ardupilot, fixed wing (Arduplane) has an autotune mode. It works very differently from the autotune of the multicopter. Before we get into the specific details of autotune for fixed wing, let's take a look at how flight modes in Arduplane work.

Fixed wing flight modes

You'll recognize many of the flight modes in the Arduplane interface from Arducopter. However, many of them work quite differently. And that's understandable. After all, a fixed-wing aircraft must keep moving to keep aloft. Here is a summary of the fixed-wing flight modes:

- **MANUAL**: Consider this making the airplane dumb. In this mode, Pixhawk's features are essentially off. You're flying the airplane as you would any other RC aircraft.
- **STABILIZE**: This mode offers basic stabilization. You're still flying the plane on manual control, but Pixhawk will make minor corrections for turbulence and wind. Also, upon releasing the sticks, the airplane will level itself out.
- **Fly By Wire_A (FBWA)**: This is the most popular assisted flight mode. In this mode, the airplane cannot be inverted (no loops or rolls). The pitch and roll are limited by the parameters (LIM_ROLL_CD in centidegrees, and LIM_PITCH_MAX/LIM_PITCH_MIN) in mission planner. The throttle is still completely controlled by the pilot, so it is still possible to stall the aircraft. However, the throttle is limited by the THR_MIN and THR_MAX settings.
- **Fly By Wire_B (FBWB)**: Not many pilots use FBWB because it's a bit of a different flying technique from traditional piloting. In this mode, when sticks are centered, the airplane maintains altitude. Rather than elevator controls affecting the pitch, it merely tells the autopilot to climb or descend. This is limited by the FBWB_CLIMB_RATE parameter (in meters per second). Whether pulling back or pushing forward on the elevator control makes the plane go up or down is controlled by the FBWB_ELEV_REV parameter. The default is pulling back to climb.
- **AUTOTUNE**: This mode allows you to fly the aircraft and automatically set the PID values for stabilized modes. There are some tricks to it, and we'll get to the full process in just a moment.
- **TRAINING**: Training mode is perfect for those who are new to flying and is designed to teach new pilots how to fly RC aircraft in **MANUAL** mode. It gives the pilot full control and offers no stabilization. However, it does limit the roll angle of the aircraft. It also calculates the airspeed needed during turns, and does not allow us to roll beyond the point of possible tip stalls.
- **Acrobatic (ACRO)**: Acro is a stabilized mode, but with a manual twist. Acro lets you do anything you would do in **MANUAL** mode (rolls, loops, and so on). However, it helps stabilize the aircraft to be more smooth in operation. It locks the current altitude of the aircraft with the sticks centered (not auto-leveling). It's a great mode for aerobatics in high winds.

- **CRUISE**: Control-wise, this mode is rather like FBWB. However, when the sticks are released, Pixhawk calculates the current trajectory and sets a waypoint 1 km away. It maintains altitude and heading toward that waypoint. You must have a GPS fix to activate this mode. You can also configure this mode to follow terrain (adjust height to account for mountains/hills automatically).

- **AUTO**: When activated, this mode begins your preplanned waypoints set in mission planner. This is fully autonomous flight. However, you can override the autonomous flight with stick inputs (which mimics FBWA mode).

- **Return to Launch (RTL)**: This is also a great mode for fail-safe operations. When activated, this mode autonomously returns the aircraft to the home point (where the aircraft was launched from). It will then loiter at an altitude set by the `ALT_HOLD_RTL` parameter until further instructions. You must have a GPS fix to activate this mode.

- **LOITER**: In this mode, the plane will automatically circle around the place where you activated the loiter mode. The radius of the circle is controlled by `WP_LOITER_RAD`, but will not exceed the `NAV_ROLL_CD` limits. Additionally, it is constrained by the `NAVL1_PERIOD` parameter. This mode is also only available with a GPS fix.

- **CIRCLE**: Circle is similar to loiter, but does not rely on a GPS fix. For this reason, it will not necessarily stay circling over the same area. If winds are in effect, the circle may slowly move downwind. It's generally used as a fail-safe (circle for a period, then RTL). The circle is also quite large as the bank angle is 1/3 of the `LIM_ROLL_CD` parameter to make sure that the plane can stay stable without a GPS fix.

- **GUIDED**: This is the mode you would use as a click-to-fly mode on a laptop. It facilitates clicking on a point on a map without predefining a mission in the mission planner. The plane will then fly to the spot on the map that was clicked on and loiter there awaiting further instructions. Additionally, if geo-fencing is enabled and that fence is breached, the aircraft will automatically enter this mode and return to the predefined return point.

- **TAKEOFF**: This is for advanced users only. Do not attempt automatic takeoffs with your first plane, nor with any plane until it is sufficiently tuned. Auto takeoff is set by a mission script only. The plane will increase throttle to the `THR_MAX` parameter, and ascend to a target altitude set by your mission parameters. The plane will attempt to maintain the heading it is pointed at before the mode is initiated down the runway, and until altitude is reached. If it is a hand-launched (or catapult launched) aircraft, the `TKOFF_THR_MINACC` and `TKOFF_THR_MINSPD` parameters are used to determine when to throttle-up based on velocity.

- **LAND**: Like **TAKEOFF** mode, this mode is not for the faint of heart and can only be set using the mission scripting. When approaching the landing point designated by the mission, the plane will slow and descend autonomously. Once either a flare altitude (set by LAND_FLARE_ALT) or a time to target in seconds (set by LAND_FLARE_SEC) the plane will flare to a pitch set by LAND_PITCH_CD (in centidegrees) and hold heading until touchdown. It's a very tricky process to get this mode set up just right.

As you can see, there are a plethora of flight modes to choose from that will fit just about any of your needs. But before you can use most of them, you need to be tuned up.

Setting flight modes

For your first few flights, you're really only concerned with three flight modes-**Manual**, **FBWA**, and **AUTOTUNE**. So, we've set up those modes on a 3-position selector switch as modes 1, 2, and 3 as shown in the following screenshot:

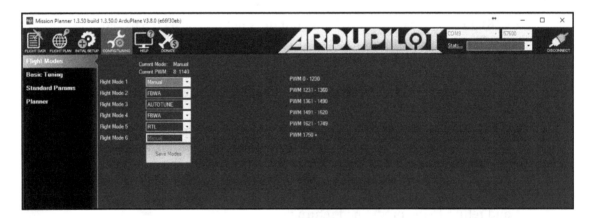

By flipping another switch on the remote, we'll have access to modes 4, 5, and 6. But for our first few flights, we won't even worry about these. Right now we just want **Manual**, **FBWA**, and **AUTOTUNE**.

Autotune level

The autotune level (AUTOTUNE_LEVEL) determines how aggressive the final handling of your aircraft will be. The higher the number, the more severe the responsiveness of the plane. The lower the number, the lazier and more sluggish a plane will respond. Numbers above 6 should only be attempted by very experienced pilots as they are not very forgiving and require a great deal of finesse while piloting the plane. The default setting is 6 (as shown in the following screenshot):

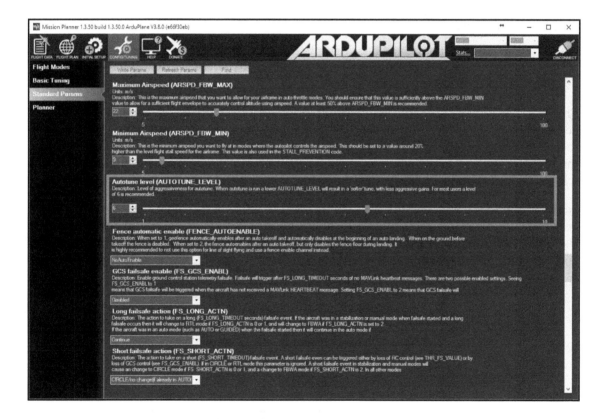

The tuning process

Every airframe is different. Sometimes even the same model airframe can have different settings from one airplane to the next. So, it's important to know that any settings you see for PIDs are not the settings you should use for your plane. Rather, this section is about the process of how to arrive at those PID settings. The first step is to make sure your airplane flies right with no Pixhawk input whatsoever.

Your maiden flight

Maidening an aircraft just means taking it into the air for the first time. The big difference between maidening a Pixhawk airplane and any other RC aircraft is that you should never use the trim controls on your radio.

Trim controls on the radio are small buttons or sliders near the sticks that allow a user to adjust the control surfaces in real time for straight flight by offsetting the value (PWMs) of the sticks. The problem is that by offsetting the values of the sticks by using trim controls, the Pixhawk will not know when the sticks are centered. And thus, several flight modes will not work properly.

So, what would we do to get the plane to fly straight without trim controls on the radio? An arduous task of mechanical trimming by altering the length of the push rods that connect the servos to the control surfaces. The following diagram shows the two types of push rods and how they are adjusted:

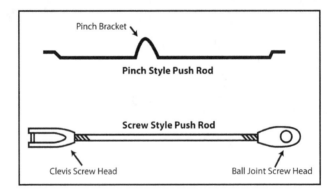

As you can see, there are essentially two types of push rods. The pinch style rod uses a crimped bracket to change the length of the rod. Pinching the pinch bracket more shortens it while spreading it will lengthen the rod. The screw style rod is much more rigid and will either have clevis heads, or ball joint receptacle heads to attach to the control points or servos.

Before your first flight, all of these rods should be adjusted so that when the servos are zeroed (turned on with the sticks centered) all surfaces should be even with the shapes of the wing, vertical stabilizer, or horizontal stabilizer.

During your flight(s), if the plane drifts (yaw, pitch, or roll) you should land, then adjust the push rods and try again. It's a tedious task and very time consuming. By the time you have all your control surfaces trimmed out, you should be able to center the sticks and the plane should fly straight and level (barring any outside forces such as wind or turbulence).

All in all, it could take several hours to get your control surfaces trimmed. Once your plane is trimmed out, you're ready to move to the next step.

AUTOTUNE flight

This is the first time you're going to allow Pixhawk to take control of your plane. Understand that when you are in any mode other than manual you are no longer truly flying the plane. Pixhawk is actively taking control of your plane and graciously allowing some of your commands to be forwarded on to the servos. The only way to truly take back control of the plane is with **MANUAL** mode. This is your ultimate fail safe. So always be prepared to switch into manual (especially during the tuning process).

Taking off and getting ready to tune

AUTOTUNE mode is very much like **FBWA** mode (in how the plane handles). So, after taking off in **MANUAL** mode, make sure the plane is flying straight and level. Then, switch into **FBWA** mode (and be ready to switch back to manual). If the plane suddenly dives, rises, or rolls, switch back to manual and land. This means that your Pixhawk was not properly levelled. You'll want to set the level again in Pixhawk's mission planner.

Entering AUTOTUNE

Once you're feeling somewhat comfortable in **FBWA** mode, you're ready to switch to **AUTOTUNE**. Make sure you are flying on a full battery for auto-tuning. It requires a lot of flight to make sure it is as accurate as possible. Here are the main points about what happens when you switch into **AUTOTUNE**:

- Upon activation, Pixhawk will set default values for your PIDs (found on the tuning page of mission planner). These values are dependent upon your AUTOTUNE_LEVEL.
- Pixhawk will constantly monitor your pitch and roll rates to see if they exceed 80% of your maximum rates set in mission planner. You will use your sticks to help Pixhawk learn how your aircraft behaves using this.
- Every 10 seconds, new rates will be saved based on the monitoring of your aircraft by Pixhawk. In other words, if your aircraft becomes unstable, you have 10 seconds to switch to manual and cancel the current rates. It's kind of like an undo feature.
- Starting with the default, Pixhawk rates will make your aircraft seem sluggish. But as you progress with **AUTOTUNE** mode, you'll notice the handling getting better and better. Make sure you have plenty of room, because at first this will mean very wide and slow turns.

How to fly in AUTOTUNE

AUTOTUNE is not a subtle process. Anyone watching the airplane will think you may be flying under the influence. It's dependent upon extreme movements on the sticks so that Pixhawk knows how to react to extreme circumstances.

First, you'll want to tune ailerons, then elevators (roll, then pitch). To do this, just move the aileron control full left quickly. This will make the aileron move to maximum deflection. Hold it there for a minimum of 2 seconds. Don't worry, the plane will not roll over. It will stop its bank at the maximum bank angle we had set before. Then, quickly move the stick to the right and hold it there for a minimum of another 2 seconds. After moving both left and right you have completed one cycle.

With each cycle the tuning improves by roughly 5%. The Pixhawk manual states that you should do 20 full cycles. However, doing more does improve the tuning. So, I suggest a minimum of 30 cycles (but find myself doing 40-50 any time I am doing an **AUTOTUNE**).

If you find yourself running low on battery at any point during AUTOTUNE, it's ok. Just remember to wait the full 10 seconds for the parameters currently in memory to be saved before switching out of **AUTOTUNE**. Land in **MANUAL** mode, replace the battery, and pick up from where you left off.

After the roll is tuned, move on to pitch tuning. This is done the same way. Full elevator control back for a minimum of 2 seconds, followed by full elevator forward for a minimum 2 seconds. Again, this is a full cycle and should be done a minimum of 30 times. After all tuning is complete in **AUTOTUNE**, remember to wait the 10 seconds for the parameters to be saved and land in **MANUAL** mode.

Ok, great! So now the airplane is all tuned up, right? Wrong. There's still a lot left to do.

Testing AUTOTUNE

Before we move on to the next step, let's make sure that the **AUTOTUNE** settings are nice and smooth. After all, the next step is a fully autonomous flight. The first thing we'll want to make sure is that the aircraft doesn't lose any altitude during turns. Take off in **MANUAL** mode and initiate **FBWA** mode. Generally, some elevator is required during turns to keep the plane from losing altitude. So, try a tight turn by only moving the ailerons to the left or right and let the plane circle. If it loses altitude (or gains), an adjustment needs to be made. Land in **MANUAL** mode, and adjust the PTCH2SRV_RLL parameter. This is how much elevator Pixhawk mixes in during a turn. If it loses altitude, increase the value, and try again. If it gains, decrease the value. Do this in 0.05 increments (so 1.0 may become 1.05, and so on). If you need to go above 1.3 or below 0.8, something is wrong and you should either retune Pixhawk, or re-examine the setup for problems, which could include a bad CG.

While you're in the air, get into straight and level flight, and note a comfortable flying speed. Then, set your cruise speed to this value after you land. Also while in the air, get into straight and level flight and slowly start backing off the throttle. Note when the plane starts becoming unstable. Increase slowly until the plane is stable again, and make note of this speed. This speed value should be set as your minimum airspeed value. And finally, do the same with increasing the speed. If the plane becomes irratic, back off and note the highest possible stable speed as the maximum airspeed value.

Now that we've verified the smoothness of the flight, it's time to take the training wheels off!

Autopilot tune

The many uses for autopilot depend on the airplane to fly in a straight line and execute turns as tightly as possible. For instance, mapping using a fixed wing requires an airplane to fly in rows of straight lines that are fairly close together. If a turn is too large, or the plane can't fly a straight line, there may be gaps in the map, and that means a very poor map indeed. Take a turn too tight, and you could end up with similar issues, or even blow the wings right off the plane (by pulling too many Gs).

So, the final stage of flight tuning is to make sure the aircraft can fly in a straight line and execute (reasonably) tight turns.

Setting up the mission

Before even connecting (via telemetry) to your plane, you should set up a rectangular mission (as shown in the following screenshot). It's important to have long straightaways so that you can see the actual ability of the plane to adhere to a straight line:

The first thing you'll notice is that this rectangle is actually 5 points with 6 entries in the **Waypoints** window (bottom). I'm sure there's a logic to it, but mission planner does not allow you to simply add a repeat behavior to the end of a mission. Instead, you need to create an extra waypoint at the end as a dummy waypoint, and insert a DO_JUMP behavior just before that extra waypoint.

The DO_JUMP behavior cycles to a specified waypoint number in the list. Here's a closer look at the **Waypoints** window:

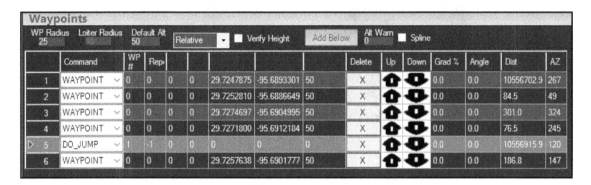

We highlighted the DO_JUMP behavior. Notice that it is 5th on the list. So, by executing this command, number 6 (the 5th waypoint) is never used. The dropdown in the Command column is where we select the type of command. Landing, takeoff, loiter, and many other options are available here. The command is inserted by selecting number 4, and clicking on the **Add Below** button (top).

You can also see that under the WP# column, the number 1 is entered. This tells Pixhawk which command number (left column) to execute. In this case, go back to the beginning (number 1). Finally, the only other column to be concerned about with this behavior is the Repeat column (just right of the WP# column). Here, you can tell Pixhawk how many times to loop through the command list before moving on to the next command after DO_JUMP. Entering -1 means that the loop will repeat infinitely (until you switch out of autopilot mode; thus, command 6 is never reached).

Now, let's take a closer look at waypoints. The following screenshot shows the same flight plan with a waypoint highlighted:

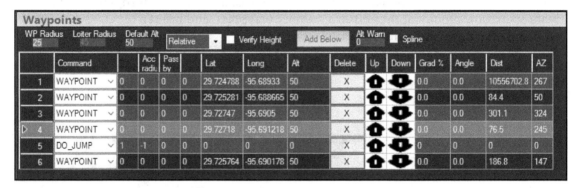

	Command		Acc radiu	Pass by	Lat	Long	Alt	Delete	Up	Down	Grad %	Angle	Dist	AZ
1	WAYPOINT	0	0	0	0	29.724788	-95.68933	50	X			0.0	0.0	10556702.8	267
2	WAYPOINT	0	0	0	0	29.725281	-95.688665	50	X			0.0	0.0	84.4	50
3	WAYPOINT	0	0	0	0	29.72747	-95.6905	50	X			0.0	0.0	301.1	324
4	WAYPOINT	0	0	0	0	29.72718	-95.591218	50	X			0.0	0.0	76.5	245
5	DO_JUMP	1	-1	0	0	0	0	0	X			0	0	0	0
6	WAYPOINT	0	0	0	0	29.725764	-95.690178	50	X			0.0	0.0	186.8	147

Above the table: **Waypoints** — WP Radius 25, Loiter Radius, Default Alt 50, Relative, Verify Height, Add Below, Alt Warn 0, Spline

As you can see, when you highlight a waypoint row, many of the column headings change. For some of these, it's because the actual column for that type of command serves a different function.

The main column to concern yourself with on waypoints is the Alt column. This is the altitude of the waypoint. Because all of our altitudes are at 50 meters, the Grade % and the Angle columns stay at 0.0. These columns are helpful to let you know if your plane can make the climb or not.

A very important parameter on the waypoints screen to set is the WP Radius (top-left of the Waypoints window). It's very important to set this radius to larger than the tightest turn radius (that you set during tuning) possible of your drone. In the preceding screenshot, you can see that we set ours to 25 (meters).

The following screenshot shows the **Write WPs** button (**Write Waypoints**) on the right side of the mission planner interface. Connect to your plane's Pixhawk, and write the waypoints to it using this button. That's right... Pixhawk saves the waypoints on the module aboard the plane. The ground station is not sending each waypoint to Pixhawk... it's driving itself:

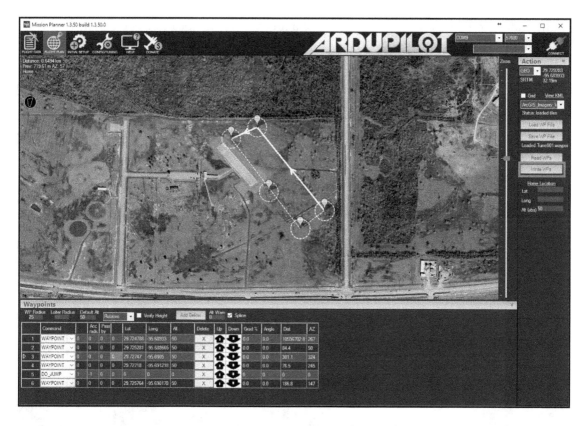

Go back to your flight mode settings now, and set up one mode to FBWB, and another to Auto. Make sure you still have a **MANUAL** mode ready to go if something goes wrong. That's it we're ready to tune autopilot.

Flying the tuning mission

Time to do it. The culmination of this whole chapter. Time to finalize the tuning of your plane. You're not ready to take off just yet. Once you get to your flying field, park the plane in the takeoff position, power it up, and connect to your Pixhawk via telemetry. We need to set the home point.

Right under the Write WPs button, you'll see a link for Home Location, click on it. This will set the home location on the map to the current coordinates (as shown in the following screenshot):

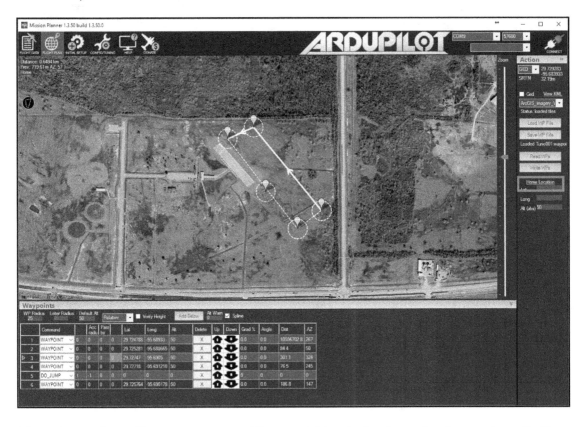

Now, we need to calibrate our sensors. The good thing is that it can be done automatically at the touch of a button. Back on the Flight Data screen, you'll notice (in the following screenshot) that we have our **Actions** screen open (lower-left). By choosing **PREFLIGHT_CHECKLIST** from the dropdown, and selecting the **Do Action** button next to it, Pixhawk will calibrate the barometer, the air speed indicator for the current air pressure of your flight area, and the day you're flying. Just throw a cloth over the front of the plane to cover the pitot tube before running this function (else, any wind will affect the calibration):

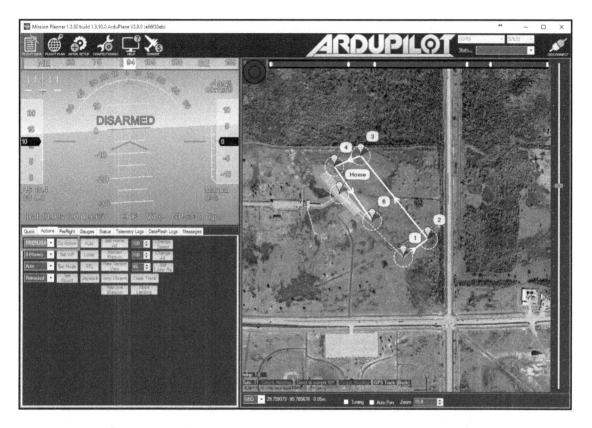

Ok, so it's go time. Launch the plane again (in **MANUAL** mode). Once it's up to roughly our altitude of the first waypoint, flip the mode into **FBWB**. In this closest pilot-controlled mode to full autopilot, fly for a short while. This is your last check that you have your other tuning parameters ready. If the plane is stable, flip the mode to Auto. This will engage the autopilot, and the plane will wait for a moment, and then make its first turn toward the first waypoint.

As it moves along its path, you'll see that the flight path (purple) will look something like the following image:

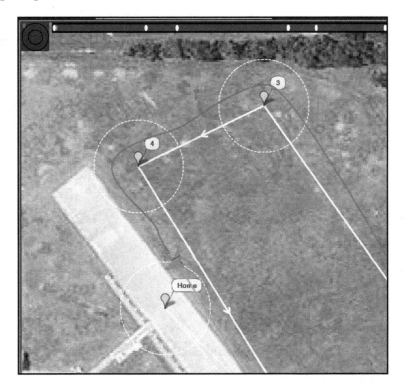

As you can see, the plane is traveling a bit outside the line between waypoints. This will always happen with a fixed wing plane due to the nature of the beast. However, we do want to get it as close as possible to that line. The way to do this is to make the turning radius as tight as possible without making the airplane unstable. The first sign of instability is if the airplane oscillates its yaw (fishtails).

You can actually make this adjustment while the plane is in the air. Hand your flight control over to another trusted pilot (in case something goes wrong, you want them to be able to flip to manual and land the plane), and switch to the **Basic Tuning** screen as shown in the following screenshot:

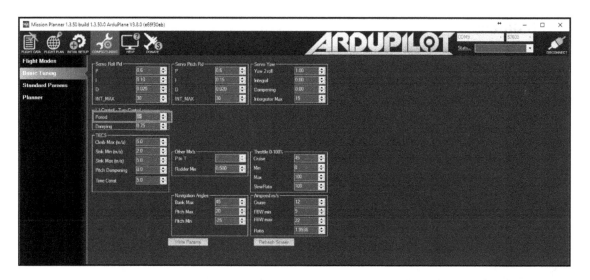

If the plane is flying too loose (outside of the path by too much), reduce the **Period** parameter of the **L1 Control** area by 1. It may be tedious, but you must make small increments in this process, or you risk crashing your plane. If it's too tight (fishtailing), increase the number by 1. Keep this process going until you get the flight path as tight as possible without fishtailing. Don't forget, every time you change the value to click on the write params button in the interface.

After this calibration is done, go ahead and land the plane (in **MANUAL** mode). That's it! Your basic tuning is done. Now, let's look at something a bit more advanced.

Auto-landing tuning

Before attempting an auto-landing, make several flights in autopilot with your plane. Make sure that you are completely happy with the way it flies. Landing is by far the most difficult part of flying. A poorly tuned plane puts you at a huge disadvantage when attempting automatic landing, and nearly guarantees a crash.

During normal autopilot, you can get away with not tuning the **Total Energy Control System** (TECS). If it sounds complicated it is. Basically, this system manages the throttle to climb/descent ratios to keep the aircraft capable of maintaining a fairly constant airspeed during climbs, ascents, and level flight. This system is crucial for auto-landing, so it should certainly be tuned before attempting it. Let's take a look at it in the upcoming section.

TECS tuning

First, you should have a stable tune as outlined earlier for your aircraft before doing TECS tuning. This is a process where you'll need two people: One pilot and another person watching the telemetry from the aircraft (specifically the airspeed most of the time). All of these settings need to be altered in the parameter list.

Here are the initial steps (use FBWA mode for this):

1. Set the maximum throttle percentage (THR_MAX). This is the throttle required to still climb at your set cruise speed (TRIM_ARSPD_CM) at your maximum pitch angle (default 20 degrees). The default of 75% works for most aircraft. But lower speed craft may require more, while ballistic aircraft (which can climb straight up) may require less. Fly at the maximum pitch and find a comfortable spot. Have your ground station monitor call out your airspeed and change it using the THR_MAX setting to that number.

2. Set the throttle for cruising (TRIM_ARSPD_CM) during level flight using the TRIM_THROTTLE parameter. This can be done by flying in FBWA mode and testing different settings.

3. Set the minimum and maximum airspeed limits. Maximum (ARSPD_FBW_MAX) should be set at the air speed achieved when at THR_MAX during level flight. Minimum (ARSPD_FBW_MIN) should be set at the slowest speed you can fly at without stalling or losing stability.

4. Set the maximum pitch angle (LIM_PITCH_MAX). Now that you've set THR_MAX, test it in FBWA mode. Go to max throttle and climb as hard as you can. If your airspeed exceeds the TRIM_ARSPD during the climb, either increase LIM_PITCH_MAX or decrease THR_MAX. If your airspeed falls below ARSPD_FBW_MIN during the climb, then either reduce LIM_PITCH_MAX, or increase THR_MAX. Ideally, you want a balance so that at max throttle in FBWA at maximum climb rate, you maintain the airspeed target at TRIM_ARSPD.

5. Set the minimum pitch angle (LIM_PITCH_MIN). This is set to how much you can pitch the nose down while at THR_MIN without over speeding your aircraft.

6. Set the maximum climb rate (TECS_CLMB_MAX). Don't confuse this with airspeed or pitch. This is strictly how fast the aircraft gains altitude. Set this to the fastest rate you can possibly climb at THR_MAX and an airspeed equaling TRIM_ARSPD_CM.

7. Set the minimum sink rate (TECS_SINK_MIN). Set this to the rate of descent when your throttle is set to THR_MIN, and the sink rate when you pitch the nose down and can maintain an airspeed equaling TRIM_ARSPD_CM.

8. Set the maximum sink rate (TECS_SINK_MAX). This is figured by descending the aircraft without exceeding the lower pitch limit and never exceeding the ARSPD_FBW_MAX.

Testing and fine tuning TECS

You'll need to test your tune and dial it in before moving on to setting up autonomous landing. Here are the steps for testing:

1. Set the aircraft into a loiter around your home point using RTL. Make sure that it's able to maintain altitude without a variance greater than 10 m. If it begins to oscillate height, increase the TECS_TIME_CONST. Increase by only 1 at a time. If you find yourself making an overall change of 10 or more, you'll need to go all the way back and check your original PID tuning.

2. Check that the balance between THR_MAX, TECS_CLIMB_MAX, and LIM_PITCH_MAX is correct. Simply send a command for the aircraft to increase altitude by about 60 m while in loiter around RTL. Throttle should go to around 80% of THR_MAX, and the pitch should be around 5° less than LIM_PITCH_MAX. Here's how to troubleshoot any issues:

    1. If the speed begins dropping below what you are comfortable with or the throttle is pegged at THR_MAX; either increase THR_MAX, or reduce TECS_CLIMB_MAX.

    2. The pitch angle is pegged at maximum constantly; either increase LIM_PITCH_MAX or reduce TECS_CLIMB_MAX.

3. Check the balance between LIM_PITCH_MIN and TECS_CLMB_MIN. Send a command for the plane to descend by about 60 m while in loiter around RTL. Optimally, the throttle will decrease and hold at THR_MIN, and the airspeed stays below ARSPD_FBW_MAX, while LIM_PITCH_MIN stays about 5° above its setting. Here's how to troubleshoot it if these requirements are not met:

    1. If the pitch is pegged at the LIM_PITCH_MIN, either reduce the TECS_SINK_MAX, or reduce the LIM_PITCH_MIN number.

    2. If the speed is too fast, then decrease the TECS_SINK_MAX

There are still other parameters you can use to fine tune the TECS. Generally though, you won't need these except in special cases. For a complete list of parameters, go to this page: `http://ardupilot.org/plane/docs/tecs-total-energy-control-system-for-speed-heig ht-tuning-guide.html#complete-parameter-list`.

Now that TECS is tuned, we can start setting up our autonomous landing parameters.

Auto-landing setup and parameters

Luckily, there aren't a ton of parameters for auto-landing itself. Unfortunately though, getting these just right can be a frustrating process. Let's take a look at them one by one:

- `LAND_FLARE_SEC` and `LAND_FLARE_ALT`: We'll cover both of these at the same time as they are very closely related. `LAND_FLARE_SEC` is given first priority of the two, and this is simply the number of seconds before impact with the ground that the plane should flare. Flaring is cutting power, and pitching the nose up to slow the plane and start final descent to the landing zone. `LAND_FLARE_ALT` is how many meters from the ground the airplane should perform this same task. If you are relying solely on Pixhawk's barometer for altitude, this set of numbers should be fairly high (such as 10 seconds and 6 meters). Since we're using a fairly accurate rangefinder, we set this to 4 seconds and 2 meters.

- `TECS_LAND_SPDWGT`: This is a parameter to control the balance between the landing airspeed (we'll cover that in a moment), and the glide slope between the last waypoint, and the landing target. The glide slope should never go above 10% (for example, descending 30m from 300m away), and ideally would be much lower than that. But if your landing speed is close to stall, you would want to give more priority to airspeed than to glide slope. The range is 0-2. 1 is an equal balance (default). 0 gives complete priority to glide slope, and 2 gives complete priority to speed. You may use decimals (float) for these values. A value of -1 gives dynamic scaling of this value, constantly adjusting the priority until it is at 0 on touch down. It tends to yield more accurate landings.

- `TECS_LAND_ARSPD`: This is the speed that you wish to land at. Ideally, this is a speed at which you are not stalling, but are losing altitude.

- `LAND_PF_ALT` and `LAND_PF_SEC`: These settings are similar to flare. However, these are preflare. By preflaring, the aircraft can drop its speed below the `TECS_LAND_ARSPD` and actually accelerate to the landing speed. This can give you greater control during landing for Pixhawk to work with. These values should be larger than those of the flare settings (for instance, if `LAND_FLARE_ALT` is 4, `LAND_PF_ALT` should be 6 or even 8).

- LAND_PF_ARSPD: This is the target velocity for your preflare airspeed. It should be below the TECS_LAND_ARSPD setting, but above stall speed. Some aircraft land very fast (such as EDF jets) in which case a setting of 1 will simply tell the aircraft to bleed off as much speed as possible before reaching the flare zone.
- TECS_LAND_SINK: This is the descent speed for touchdown. By default, it is set to 0.25 meters per second, which works for many models. However, if your aircraft bounces, you'll want to reduce this further.
- LAND_PITCH_CD: This is the minimum target pitch for the flare. Aircraft with tricycle landing gear (one in the front, two in the back) will want this to be around 300 (3° because CD in a parameter means centidegrees).
- TECS_LAND_DAMP: This is a dampener on the rate of pitch changes during the flare. Sudden and extreme movements during near-stall speeds are dangerous, so this setting can be handy. Larger numbers mean more dampening.
- LEVEL_ROLL_LIMIT: Used to control the maximum roll angle (default 5°) after the flare. This is to prevent the wings from hitting the ground during landing. Because of this, during extreme crosswinds, the plane may not be able to land on the desired target.
- TECS_LAND_SRC: This parameter is used to adjust your TECS_LAND_SINK on the fly to make sure the plane comes down on the landing target. If you find yourself overshooting, you can decrease the number to a negative to force a stall, or force the nose down with a positive number.
- LAND_DISARMDELAY: After the plane stops moving (GPS, not airspeed), this is the delay in seconds before Pixhawk disarms. The default is 20 seconds.
- RNGFND_LANDING: This setting lets Pixhawk know whether or not to use the rangefinder to calculate distance to runway during landing. Set this to 1 if using a rangefinder.

Ok, maybe there are quite a few settings. But the main ones you'll use for tuning are the ones affecting the flares.

The testing

Set up a mission with the final waypoint low enough so that landing won't produce a glide slope greater than 8%, nor less than 5%, and a DO_LAND_START marker on your landing zone. Remember to give yourself some safe space before and after the landing zone (in case of under or over shoots).

Then, flip into automode with your finger hovering over the switch to go back to manual and watch the plane very closely. Be ready to flip to manual and go to full power and ascend back to the sky.

If you don't like the way it lands, use the settings mentioned earlier to adjust your flares and speeds and angles to counteract what you don't like. Of course, land in **MANUAL** mode before making the adjustments and try again.

It will take several iterations before you feel comfortable with the landing. Once you do, add a `TAKEOFF` command to the beginning of your mission, and see if you can run a fully autonomous flight from takeoff to landing. If you succeed, you will be very happy.

Summary

WOW! That was a lot, right? Now you can see why fixed wing aircrafts really are the holy grail of drone designers. In this chapter, we've learned about the extra components needed to integrate Pixhawk into a fixed wing drone. We've learned about placement, and thinking through the design. And finally, we went through the very complex and drawn-out process of tuning a fixed wing drone.

In the next chapter, we're not actually going to build a drone. Instead, we're going to walk you through some concepts of creating a VTOL aircraft... FUN!

8
The Principles of VTOL with Pixhawk

Designing and tuning a **Vertical Takeoff and Landing** (**VTOL**) aircraft can take a very long time. It may even take years to design and get your VTOL aircraft set up and working with stability. Originally, this chapter was going to be based on something fun—a *Battlebot* design. But, when the book was announced, one thing was very clear. You (the readers) wanted to know more about VTOL. So, without the time nor budget to create a VTOL prototype aircraft (by the time we have made one work properly, it's likely a new version of Pixhawk would be released); we're going to work on the principle and theory of how someone would create a Pixhawk VTOL; not how someone did create a Pixhawk VTOL.

In this chapter, we will cover the following topics:

- The types of VTOL aircraft
- Limitations and considerations of VTOL
- Fusing a multicopter and fixed wing design
- Tuning a VTOL aircraft

The types of VTOL

There are essentially two types of VTOL: hybrid and vectored. All other VTOLs are a variation of the two. One is far easier to build, and one flies much better (and more efficiently). Unfortunately though, these are not the qualities of the same type of VTOL.

The hybrid VTOL

This is certainly easy to design and build. It's just a matter of taking a very good airplane and attaching a multirotor frame to it (centred around the CG of the airplane). That's a bit of an oversimplification, but accurate. Unfortunately, with this type of design the multicopter propellers themselves can begin spinning during forward flight due to the wind. And even with no spinning they are essentially control surfaces and can cause strange turbulence and vortices around the wings, which alters the way it flies. This, plus having surfaces designed around moving air that are non-functional during forward flight, will reduce your efficiency. And (in general) making a fixed wing drone is about trying to gain more flight time (and possibly speed). So creating wind resistance is counter-productive. The following image shows a hybrid VTOL aircraft:

Thrust vectored VTOL

Thrust vectoring is just a fancy word for changing the direction of the air that the thrust system is pushing. Whether it's by rotating propellers (like the Osprey military aircraft), rotating jet vents (like a Harrier), or changing the whole direction of the aircraft (like the X-Plane drone, which lands and takes off on its tail as a quad, and rotates to fly forward), the way to recognize a thrust vectored VTOL is that it uses the same thrust system to land and take off vertically as for pushing the aircraft forward during flight.

It's much more difficult to get this right during the design phase, from changes in the CG to taking into account how pushing or pulling an airplane through the air affects the airplane mode flight in different ways. It's certainly a design challenge, and you need to have a budget. Count on several crashes during the transition to forward flight on this type of aircraft until you get it right.

The reward for all of your effort with a vectored thrust VTOL is that every bit of weight is utilized during all modes of flight. You don't have any *non-functional* parts just hanging out during airplane flight. This also means no wasted energy. Whether that's pushing parts through the wind that aren't used during forward flight, or using control surfaces to counteract the way they affect your flight. Every time you (or your flight controller) uses a control surface, that means resistance from the wind, and of course, that means reducing the flight time.

The following image is a Harrier. The US (and British) Navies use this aircraft heavily due to its ability to land and take off from much smaller aircraft carriers that are far less expensive to build than the larger ones that carry aircraft that require a catapult to launch, and trap wires to land. The Harrier uses a large turbofan jet engine, and vents the exhaust of this engine to nozzles under the wings (on the sides of the main hull) that rotate, and have louvers to even push thrust to the sides. It's a very typical example of a vectored thrust VTOL aircraft, and one of the first:

The Hawker Harrier; image courtesy of Wikimedia commons

There are many variations of both of these types of aircraft, and even combinations of the two. For instance, the F-35 Lightning vectors the nozzle for its main jet down and a hatch opens above (and below) the aircraft for a second turbofan to provide lift to the front of the aircraft during VTOL operations. When in airplane mode, these hatches close and the turbofan turns off. So, although the aircraft's wind resistance efficiency is not affected during forward flight, the extra weight must still be carried. Some drones have quad propellers and motors that extend and retract when changing mode, and there are yet other types of variants and combinations. But essentially, thrust vectoring and hybrid are the two main types of VTOL.

Designing your first VTOL

VTOLs have all the complexity of an airplane and a multicopter combined. So, you may want to start simple. Remember the Bixler we fitted with Pixhawk in the last chapter? This would be an excellent candidate to start with. Why? Because it's already a fully set up airplane. So, the first half is already done. Now we just have to figure out how to hybridize it.

We need to integrate the functionality of a multicopter without adding too much weight to the frame. So, it's not just a matter of gluing on a multicopter airframe. The multicopter needs to lift the weight of the airplane, and the airplane needs to keep the weight of the multicopter aloft during forward flight.

Not only that, but the energy requirements for our airplane are not very high (using just a 3S 1100 mAh LiPo battery). We could easily lift a drone and the airplane's weight with a 6S LiPo battery. But then we have all the extra weight of the battery, and all the extra weight of the motors and propellers to lift that battery. The airframe of the airplane could not keep this in the air very well (and the wings may even break off in turns), not to mention that the motor and ESC are sure to not only burn out, but probably catch fire if a 6S is applied to them. So, we'll need a bigger ESC and a bigger motor for the plane as well (even more weight).

And remember, this is the simple design.

The challenge

Luckily, we know just how much the plane already weighs wet (wet is with battery). That weight is 34.79 ounces (986.28 grams). What we need to do is find multicopter motors, ESCs, spars, and wiring that is under the flying weight limit for a multicopter with the total wet weight (of plane and additional parts) with enough juice left in the battery to maintain forward flight for a reasonable amount of time, and then land again vertically. We also need to stay below the maximum weight of the Bixler.

Our first problem arises. We're (technically) already above the maximum weight of a Bixler. The published maximum flying weight is 650 grams (22.92 ounces). However, this appears to be a dry weight. Even so, we're already pretty much at the maximum flying weight of the Bixler. So, it's a non-starter. We need a plane with bigger wings, stronger wings, much stronger wings, and since we're going there we need something that can carry (and run on) 6S batteries: 10,000 mAh 6S batteries. This is a very common battery for moderate-to-heavy lift multicopters, and should suffice for our VTOL.

The simple gets more complex

Well, our Bixler obviously wouldn't work. It's just not designed to carry much weight nor payload for our purposes. Just one 10,000 mAh battery weighs ~1,400 grams (49.39 ounces). That's more than our entire flying weight of the Bixler. We choose this battery because 6S (22.2V) batteries provide enough juice to lift heavy loads in a multicopter. And 10,000 mAh should provide plenty of flight time for our airplane as well.

So, we know what won't do the job. What will? Enter the Skywalker EVE-2000. For a final production model, of course we'd design something more purpose built. But this is a great airframe to test out a hybrid design. It has huge wings (2,400 mm wingspan), and has a maximum wet weight of 4,600g (162.26 oz.).

The following picture is a Skywalker EVE 2000 (flown and built by Nathan Eick of Iowa):

A Skywalker EVE-2000 airplane drone flown by Nathan Eick (photo courtesy of Nathan Eick)

As you can see, it's a twin-engine plane. This presents some other design challenges. We have to extend our front rotors far enough to completely clear the propellers of the main drive system. And due to the laws of physics, that may present some leverage issues (meaning that those spars must be strong).

Another benefit to the Skywalker EVE-2000 is that it has a wooden plate inside to mount all the electronics to. If we replace that with a carbon fiber plate with some aluminum reinforcement (to keep it from flexing), this will be a perfect mounting surface to join our spars to the main hull. And that brings us to the airframe.

The (re-imagined) airframe

Let's start by just making a sketch (as before). We need to imagine how everything will fit together, then find parts and adjust our design to accommodate them:

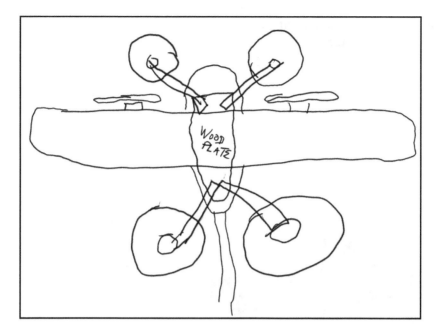

So, our idea is to go through the hull, and attach the spars directly onto the wood (replaced by carbon fiber) plate. We're going to need some hardware:

Creating our shopping list

Figuring budgets is essential when prototyping. You may be making one for a client, investors, or we're pretty sure your significant other would be interested in how much it will cost. So, it's essential before actually creating your final design to figure out what parts you'll (most likely) need.

First off, a Skywalker EVE-2000 is $285 (USD) via `fpvmodel.com`. It's a PNP (plug and play) version (so it comes with all servos, motors, and propellers), so all you need to do is plug in your Pixhawk and peripherals, then fly.

So, a Pixhawk 2.1 ($215), pitot tube ($70), and rangefinder for landing ($159) bring our running total up to $729. We're going to go a different route for GPS.

Because (generally) we want mapping data to be very accurate, we'll use a GPS system that is augmented by **Radio Telemetry Kinetics** technology (**RTK**). RTK uses a stationary GPS station on the ground and uses relation data based on the transmissions to the air system to allow the air system to get a much more accurate approximation of its actual coordinates. Where GPS has an accuracy of around a 6-foot (2-meter) diameter, RTK is centimeter accurate. That's pretty wicked-accurate. Here's the one we'd use to keep our budget and weight down:

With a price tag of $650, this brings our running total to $1,379.

With all of the variables of a multicopter, we would stop here, get it built and flight tested and tuned, and then start implementing the multicopter. But we'll get into the testing process in a bit.

Let's take the multicopter from the motors back to the airframe to make sure it can lift everything.

Many motor mounts are a bit recessed (meaning that the spar tube intersects with the plane of the motor). We want ones that are flush so that if we need to add bigger motors during testing we won't have to redesign the multicopter airframe. So, we found these:

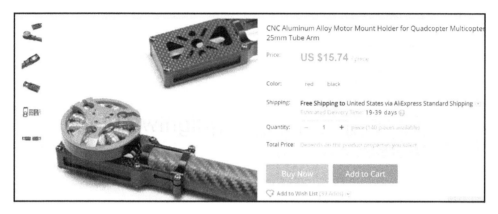

Four of these (costing ~$63) brings our total up to $1,442. They fit 25 mm carbon fiber tubes. But we'll have to wait on deciding about those because we need to know how big the propellers on the multicopter will be. We need to make sure they'll clear the airplane propellers.

Before deciding on propellers, we need to figure out the motors. Not every motor can drive every propeller. In the 6S current class, 480kv (480 rpm per volt) is a pretty safe choice. With larger props, the kv rating goes down. And with the ones we chose (in the following image), each will generate 2,000 grams of thrust when equipped with a 13" propeller with a 6.5" twist—commonly called a 13 x 6.5:

At around $120 (4 x $30), that brings our running total to $1,562. Now we look at props. We don't want folding props on a hybrid. They may fold up in the wrong way during flight, and not unfold properly when switching to multicopter mode. So, a fixed, carbon fiber prop is what we're after:

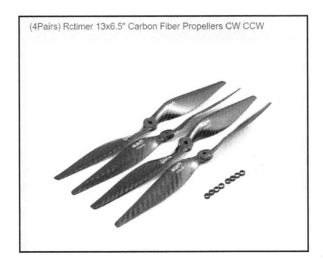

(4Pairs) Rctimer 13x6.5" Carbon Fiber Propellers CW CCW

Add another $28, and we're up to $1,590. And with a total thrust of 8,000 g, that will be plenty to lift our airplane off the ground vertically.

The motors draw ~25 A under load with those rotors, but that is sustained. Peak could shoot as high as 35. We need ESCs that can handle beyond that. If we go with 40-A ESCs, we can expect to pay around $25 each (but much higher for some brands). With that in mind, at $100 for four of them, we're now up to $1,690.

OK, now that we know we're using 13.5" (diameter) props, we know that the reach of those props is 6.75". We want some leeway, so we'll calculate the reach with clearance at 9".

Enter high school geometry, and the all-hated words Pythagorean Theorem. See? Your teachers were right! It does have uses in the real world!

We'll figure that the fuselage is ~ 9" wide, and that means we need an additional 4.5" from the center line to figure the x-axis (along the wing). We'll also figure that the prop and motor housing extend 2" from the edge of the wing on the y-axis of our triangle (going fore). If we want 9" clearance, that means $(9+4.5)^2+(9+2)^2 = (theLength)^2$. Our carbon spars need to be at least 17.42" long. That's about 442.5 mm. Let's round up to 500 mm (because we can always cut it shorter, but we can't lengthen it). We think these 20 mm (inner diameter) x 25 mm (outer diameter) x 500 mm (length) carbon fiber rods fit the bill:

Two of these (as it comes with two spars per order) brings our running total up to $1,718.

And finally, we get a carbon fiber plate 1/8" thick, 24" x 24" at $203 (from `DragonPlate.com`), and some mounting rings (four packages) at about $20 (shown in the following image). That brings our grand total to $1,941. OK, so that's our build cost. But is that what it will really cost? No. We have to build in incidentals (such as glue and the like), and the cost of tuning (in crashes). So we're going to estimate $2,500 final cost of the aircraft with no camera (to build, not what we would charge a client after all, which speaks nothing of your labour).

OK...so now that we know what parts we will be using, how do we plan to implement them?

The final plan

It's very important with a complex build like this to do more than just a sketch for how everything will lay out. Too much money is on the line to leave it to a sketch. The following image shows a three-quarter view of our final plan:

Implementing Pixhawk

In previous iterations of this type of hybrid, you would need to use PX4 firmware (rather than Ardupilot or APM) with heavy customization. Luckily, the newer Ardupilot firmware versions allow for exactly this type of VTOL (they call it a Quadplane). Obviously, the channels are going to be a little different.

The following diagram shows how all of the motors/servos are hooked up:

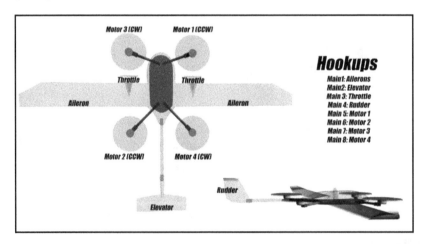

An easy way to remember motor rotational directions is that the leading edge of the propellers always turn in toward the hull on a Quadplane. Nevertheless, we marked each motor direction (CW for clockwise and CCW for counter-clockwise).

Test and tune before making the leap

With all of the quad parts on the plane, make sure that none of the quad motors have power, and connections to Pixhawk are severed. You'll want to test-fly (and probably retune) the airplane with the new parts before attempting to use the quad functionality. Make sure you have a successful tuning with the most stable flight possible.

Setting up the firmware

Unfortunately, the Quadplane feature is somewhat new. There is no wizard to set it up. In all fairness, it is such a complicated design that assuming that a user knows how to use the full parameter list is a fairly safe assumption. Luckily, the parameters to set up Quadplane are within the Arduplane firmware. So, we haven't wasted our time with the tuning of the airframe.

All of the parameters in Arduplane that are Quadplane-specific start with the letter Q. But you will only see one such parameter at first. This is Q_ENABLE.

Following is a table showing all of the parameters to get a Quadplane up and going (along with notes on them):

Parameter	Notes
Q_ENABLE	This enables the QuadPlane functionality when set to a value of 1. After setting this to 1, save and refresh the settings page to show all of the other Q parameters in the list.
Q_THR_MIN_PWM and Q_THR_MAX_PWM	These allow you to set the PWM range of the multicopter motors separately from the tractor motor (the motor tasked with providing thrust for airplane mode).
Q_A_RAT_RLL_P and Q_A_RAT_PIT_P	This is for tuning the roll and pitch rates on the P for PID values on quad mode. The default is 0.25. However, due to wind resistance and mass a higher value may be needed when tuning. You cannot autotune the multicopter mode. You must manually tune it.

ARMING_RUDDER	If you set this value to 2, it enables you to disarm your motors via the hard left rudder and throttle down. However, be careful not to fly your plane by cutting throttle to zero and ruddering hard left or you will disarm your aircraft.
Q_THR_MID	This is a value from 0-1,000; 500 is 50% throttle (and default). This is how much throttle the multicopter motors require to maintain a hover. During the tuning process, if you notice a surge in altitude during the transition to airplane mode, decrease this level. If you see a drop, increase this level.
Q_TRANSITION_MS	This is how long it takes for the Pixhawk to slowly power down the quad motors (how long to power down the motors after the minimum airspeed for lift is achieved) and vice versa. Default is 5000 (5 seconds).
ARSPD_FBW_MIN	This is the minimum airspeed for the wings to supply lift. (Triggers Q_TRANSITION_MS when reached during transitions.)
Q_VFWD_GAIN	This is set to 0 by default. If this is set to anything above zero, this is how much the tractor (airplane thrust) motor is used to help keep the multicopter level into a wind. Only use this if you're feeling advanced.
Q_ASSIST_SPEED	This parameter is used to help provide lift to the aircraft when dropping below its set speed threshold. This is not a transition to quad flight. Instead, this is still airplane flight with the quad props helping to keep the airplane from stalling.
Q_ASSIST_ANGLE	In conjunction with Q_ASSIST_SPEED, this can be very useful. Before actually stalling, an aircraft begins to lose altitude at low speeds. This is the angle of descent during level flight that the quad motors will kick in and give extra lift. During **AUTO**, **LOITER**, **RTL**, or **GUIDED** mode, the quad motors will assist with any climb rate to get the aircraft to the next waypoint (or navigation controller demanded) altitude. In FBWB, the quad motors will assist with the desired climb rate. In FBWA, the quad motors will give proportional lift based on the pilot's ascent or descent rates. This assistance is only recommended with Quadplanes that do not have enough wing-lift to maintain altitude in plane mode alone. You'll find efficiency and battery life will be significantly decreased when using this parameter.

RTL_RADIUS	This is the distance from the launch point that the aircraft turns from airplane RTL mode to VTOL **QRTL** mode (transitioning from airplane to multicopter).
Q_RTL_ALT	The altitude aimed for during QRTL mode.
Q_RTL_MODE	Set this to 1 to enable auto transitioning (using RTL_RADIUS and Q_RTL_ALT) during **RTL**.
Q_WVANE_GAIN	How actively the aircraft tries to turn into the wind during multicopter mode. Due to the nature of a VTOL airplane, the motors may need to work too hard to keep the tail from swinging around downwind. This gain allows the plane to "give in" to the wind.

Quadplanes require GPS to fly properly. Make sure you wait for the signal that you have a 3D GPS fix before attempting any flight.

Quadplane flight modes

The flight modes specific to a Quadplane are flight modes for multicopter mode. They are as follows:

- **QSTABILIZE**: Just like regular multicopter stabilize. Roll and pitch control the lean angle, but when releasing the sticks, the multicopter returns to level (but may drift). Similar to DJI's **ATTI** mode.
- **QHOVER**: Just like regular multicopter altitude hold. This holds an altitude, and you can position the multicopter using roll, pitch, and yaw controls. Releasing the sticks stops the multicopter and makes it maintain a position in a hover.
- **QLOITER**: Just like regular multicopter loiter. It's also much like **QHOVER**, but you do have control over the altitude of the aircraft. Just like DJI's **GPS** mode.
- **QLAND**: Just like regular multicopter land. This makes the vehicle descend and land regardless of its physical location. Unfortunately, this mode is not as sophisticated as multicopter landings. If there is a GPS shift while on the ground, the aircraft could tip over trying to get back to the previous location. So you should shift to **QSTABILIZE** once on the ground as this doesn't get affected by GPS drift.

- **QRTL**: Just like any **RTL** mode. Makes the vehicle return to the launch location in multicopter mode.

You should never use non-GPS modes for airplane mode. So, stay away from **ACRO**, **STABILIZE**, **MANUAL**, and **TRAINING** mode. The Pixhawk needs to be aware (constantly) of what is happening with the aircraft in Quadplane configurations. These modes could result in catastrophic results. Use **FBWA** or **FBWB** modes instead. This is a reason that you must tune your airplane before implementing Quadplane modes.

Transitioning from VTOL to airplane

Transitioning is simple once everything is tuned. All you have to do is change modes (such as going from **QLOITER** to **FBWA**). It will happen automatically. Again, avoid **MANUAL**. This will instantly cut the multicopter motors and your aircraft will drop like a rock until you manage to regain control and lift up (much like a stall).

This is what will happen when you switch to **FBWA** or **STABILIZE** from a **Q** mode (such as **QLOITER**):

1. The aircraft will attempt to maintain altitude using the quad motors and engage the airplane's tractor motor to provide thrust at user-inputted throttle.
2. Quad motors will continue to provide lift and stability until `ARSPD_FBW_MIN` airspeed is reached and if there is no pitot tube, this is based on GPS estimate.
3. `Q_TRANSITION_MS` will engage and shut down the quad motors over the specified time.

The transition back to multicopter mode works similarly, but has a few differences:

1. Airplane tractor motor will immediately stop.
2. Controls switch to multicopter mode, allowing you to maintain control via the control surfaces during glide deceleration, and multicopter motors will begin to spin up.
3. Once airspeed drops below `ARSPD_FBW_MIN`, controls switch to multicopter mode.

This procedure allows you to switch back to multicopter mode even when flying in airplane mode at high speed.

Recommended VTOL RTL procedure

There are several ways to handle **RTL** with a hybrid like this, but here's what I recommend:

1. Head back (RTL) using the airplane **RTL** mode. This gets you to the vicinity quickly.
2. Switch to **QRTL** when close to the home point. If Q_RTL_ALT, RTL_RADIUS, and Q_RTL_MODE are set, this happens automatically
3. Switch to **QLAND** and again, if Q_RTL_ALT, RTL_RADIUS, and Q_RTL_MODE are set, this will happen automatically

I find this to be the most efficient procedure. No wasting battery time on circling, or other maneuvers. Just fly in, switch modes, and land.

Notes before attempting any transitions

I know, after all that effort, you're going to be itching to see it transition. It's a long and painful road to tune your multicopter mode before even thinking of transitioning.

Make sure you adjust all of the Q tuning parameters so that the multicopter mode is flying as stable as possible before doing any hybrid flights. You'll save yourself a lot of expense and headache.

When attempting transitions, make sure you are well above a minimum height of 20 m **above ground level** (**AGL**). Until you get all of your Q transition parameters set, you are very likely to lose altitude, or even lose stability on your first tests. Even then, stay above 20 m AGL.

Summary

Well, there you have it. If we made it seem simple, we apologize. This is the absolute most complex configuration you can embark on (for the hybrid we chose the simpler "Quadplane"). If you ever choose to do a VTOL, we'd love to see your results!

In this chapter, you learned about the different types of VTOL aircraft, and how to set up the simplest flavor of VTOLs. You've learned about all of the hook-ups, design concepts, and limitations of different designs. Finally, we walked you through all of the firmware settings needed to get it to work.

In the next chapter, we'll cover some of the basics of actually digging into the firmware and settings of Ardupilot and manipulating it to customize it even further.

9
Programming Ardupilot

You can consider this chapter a quick-reference of the Mission Planner interface and parameter list. In this chapter, we're going to review the use of Mission Planner, and explain (in some cases re-explain) all of the parameters in the detailed parameter list. If you ever hit a brick wall and are looking for that specific parameter to tune, this is where you'll find it.

In this chapter, we'll cover the following topics:

- The Flight Data interface
- The Flight Plan Screen
- The Initial Setup screen
- Config/Tuning screen
- The Simulation screen
- Mission Planner Terminal

The Flight Data interface

The following image shows the flight data interface for Mission Planner:

The top-left window represents the **Heads-up Display** (**HUD**)—where you can instantly tell the orientation, altitude, and status of the aircraft. Warning messages appear as red text (such as the **DISARMED** and **Bad AHRS** warnings we see in the image).

The large window is a projected satellite map showing the location of the aircraft/multicopter/rover (in this case, a fixed wing aircraft). Protruding from the aircraft is a purple line representing the direction the aircraft is pointing at.

The window on the lower-left shows current data with several tabs to see data presented in different formats, and even transmits signals to the Pixhawk. The tabs are follows:

- **Quick**: These are the numerical values of basic telemetry data from the vehicle.
- **Actions:** This allows the user to send commands to Pixhawk such as **Loiter**, **Arm**, and so on.
- **PreFlight**: This shows a checklist and status for preflight before launching the Pixhawk vehicle. Green represents the items that are ready and red represents items which may require attention.

- **Gauges**: This shows an analog view with similar information to the quick screen. This analog view uses graphic representation in the form of virtual gauges rather than simple numbers.
- **Status**: This provides a detailed readout of every single telemetry parameter the vehicle is experiencing.
- **Telemetry Logs**: This lets the user load flight logs from Pixhawk into the computer and replay the mission to evaluate the mission post-mortem.
- **DataFlash Logs**: This is used to troubleshoot problems with Pixhawk. If you are experiencing problems with tuning or missions, these logs can be extremely useful to spot errors. Also, when asking for help from a community, the first question they'll ask is for you to provide these logs for analysis.
- **Messages**: This provides a real-time view of log entries as they happen.

The Flight Plan Screen

The following image shows the Flight Plan Screen (without fixed-wing tuning mission loaded):

The main window shows a satellite map of the mission area. The yellow lines represent the desired path of the vehicle, while the white circles represent the area for the turning arc (turning radius). The green markers represent the actual waypoint targets for the mission.

The bottom window is a chart representing all of the parameters for the mission. In this window, you can add events (such as Do Jump, which sends the vehicle back to a specific waypoint). If your camera is attached to Pixhawk, you can tell the camera to take an image/start recording. Flight modes can be set to change as well (such as "Land"). Any command Pixhawk is capable of executing can be triggered using this interface.

The window on the far right allows you to save missions for later use (to your computer), load previous missions, change the type of satellite map. Different maps can prove to be more/less detailed, and can also prove to be more/less current. Finally, at the bottom of this window, is a section that allows you to read the current waypoints loaded into Pixhawk, or write the waypoints you've just created. You must write waypoints for Pixhawk to execute the mission. The home point is also displayed here.

The Initial Setup screen

The following screenshot shows the initial setup screen's **Install Firmware** tab. This screen allows you to repurpose a Pixhawk module for other applications (such as Rover):

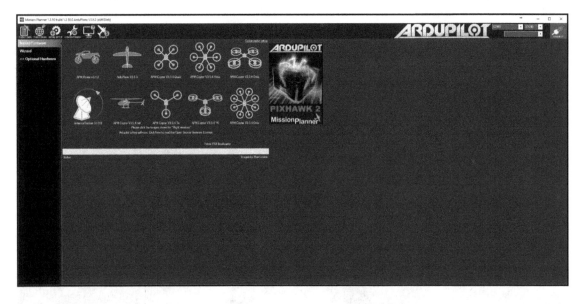

Wizard

The following screenshot shows the interface that pops up when clicking on the **Wizard** tab. This is a step-by-step configuration wizard to help get the basic setup of your Pixhawk in place:

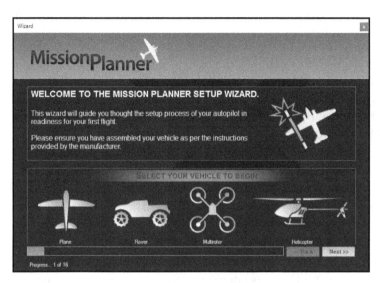

Mandatory hardware

This section allows you to calibrate/setup all of the peripherals that are required to make Pixhawk drive your vehicle properly. Let's take a look at each:

- **Accel Calibration**: This allows to calibrate the accelerometers. You'll want to do this if you are getting a **Bad AHRS** error in the Flight Data screen. Simply enter this menu and click on **Calibrate Accelerometer** to open the calibration wizard. The **Calibrate Level** button lets you calibrate the correct level position of Pixhawk. This is essential for the aircraft, otherwise they may pitch/roll when Pixhawk believes it is flying level. In multicopters, this can cause movement when trying to hover if not calibrated properly. In fixed-wings, this can cause oscillation on the pitch/roll axis if not calibrated properly. If you alter the Pixhawk location on your aircraft, this is an essential process as well.

- **Compass**: This menu allows you to calibrate your compass. When moving to a new location, it's extremely important to calibrate the compass. Even when launching from the same location, but a different time, this can be important. Sun spots, solar flares, and EM interference from environmental variables can affect the accuracy of your compass.

- **Radio Calibration**: This allows you to bind and configure your radio controller and receiver for Pixhawk. If channels are inverted (such as throttle down making the vehicle revved as if it were full throttle), you can reverse them to work properly. Also, this calibration will let Pixhawk see where middle points and limits are of your control to allow for much more stable flight/driving.

- **Calibrate ESCs**: Pixhawk will gain an understanding of how the ESCs work, and how to control the specific ESCs you are using. This section allows for the best use of your motors.

- **Flight Modes**: This allows the user to specify what modes are switched to using the flight mode switch on the controller. Note: you must click on **Save Modes** for changes to go into effect.

- **Failsafe**: This allows the user to specify which failsafe modes are active, and how to handle these modes:

    - **Battery**: This specifies what level of battery (following which) Pixhawk will execute the **Failsafe** operation

    - **Radio**: This specifies what is failsafe PWM (controller input) on throttle below which Pixhawk will execute a **Failsafe** operation

    - **GCS**: This executes **Failsafe** wherein the connection with the ground control station is lost.

Optional hardware

As the name implies, optional hardware is not crucial to the operation of a Pixhawk vehicle. However, it can (generally) improve the stability, accuracy, and/or functionality of your drone. The following are the general menus within the Optional Hardware section, and their purposes:

- **RTK/GPS Inject**: RTK and redundant GPS systems drastically improve the accuracy of positioning data. Where standard GPS accuracy is measured in meters, RTK accuracy is measured in terms of < 1cm. RTK systems are generally used for survey-grade mapping (maps that can be used for engineering). This menu section is for activating and calibrating an RTK system.

- **Sik Radio**: This allows the user to configure the radio telemetry unit(s) utilized by Pixhawk.
- **Battery Monitor (1&2)**: This allows for the configuration of the battery monitor module for Pixhawk. This includes specifying the battery capacity for the vehicle.
- **UAVCAN**: UAVCAN is a high-precision protocol for data transmission between components via a CAN bus. Timing is precisely down to the milliseconds, and large data amounts can be transmitted via this protocol. It's used primarily in large, very expensive drones and won't be used for most applications. But it's very nice to know that Pixhawk can work with it. This menu section is for enabling and configuring the UAVCAN capabilities.
- **Compass/Motor Calibration**: Motors generate EM (electro-magnetic) fields. This can affect compass accuracy. This area lets you see just how much the motors are affecting the compass, and gives you enough information to see if you should move Pixhawk/external compass.
- **RangeFinder**: This is the area where you can activate rangefinder capabilities. You should still use the parameters outlined earlier in the book to double-check the setup.
- **Airspeed**: This allows the user to activate the pitot sensor and specify its type.
- **PX4Flow**: This allows the user to activate a PX4Flow sensor. This sensor is best used on a copter (pointed down). Its purpose is to sense the ground, and maintain a hover with minimal drift by looking at the flow of pixels to keep the vehicle stationary.
- **Optical Flow**: This is pretty much the same functionality as PX4Flow. However, this is for using generic versions of optical flow sensors (rather than the precalibrated PX4Flow brand).
- **OSD**: The OSD modules display telemetry data via an overlay on top of a video transmission signal. An OSD module would be used if using either an FPV (first person view) screen or goggles (as opposed to viewing the telemetry data on a laptop screen).
- **Camera Gimbal**: This is an area for calibrating a Pixhawk-controlled camera gimbal. Unlike the **Camera Gimbal** we used in our multicopter example, this area would control the motors directly (rather than using a gimbal with a dedicated control board). This is also the area where you would enable shutter control for your camera.
- **Motor Test**: As we saw in Chapter 6, *A Simple Multicopter Drone*, this is the area where you can activate each motor of a multicopter to verify that the right motor is turning, and that it is turning in the right direction. Note that this should never be done with the propellers attached!

- **Bluetooth Setup**: An area to set up the Bluetooth module (like the one we used for the golf trolley setup). Because of its limited range, Bluetooth should not be used for aircraft or fast-moving vehicles. Keep in mind that Bluetooth has a range of about 30 metre.
- **Parachute**: This required an area to set up a parachute deployment system. These systems are not widely used, but can prove to be useful in the event of a failure of an aircraft (especially over people), or even in place of landing a vehicle. It should be noted that (especially on multicopters), the aircraft can become tangled in the parachute lines and parachutes should be viewed as the last chance, not a reliability.
- **ESP8266**: This is the area where you would setup the ESP8266 Wi-Fi module. As we discussed in our trolley chapter, this is another way of controlling/getting telemetry from your drone. Wi-Fi does have a limited range (about 100 m), but can prove to be useful (especially with Apple iOS devices which are Bluetooth prohibitive).
- **Antenna Tracker**: Longer range drones, which require a special **Beyond Visual Line of Sight** (**BLOS**) permit in the US benefit greatly from using a directional antenna, which constantly points toward a target. This is especially useful with high-quality video systems for live coverage without interference. This area is where you can set up and tune your antenna tracker.

Config/Tuning screen

As the name implies, this area is where the Pixhawk administrator would configure and tune the aircraft. Since some of these menus are only available with an advanced layout, first we'll cover the *Planner* section (which will give you access to all the advanced features).

Planner

The following screenshot shows the options for the **Planner** tab. This is the area where we configure the Mission Planner software itself:

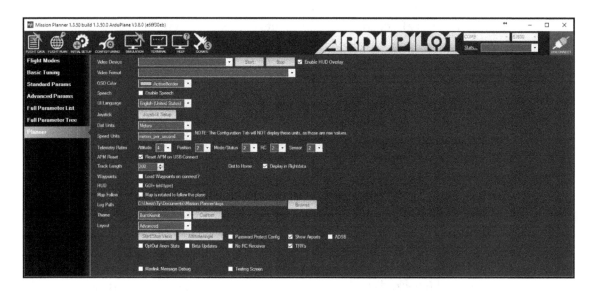

There are many options for setting up Mission Planner on your ground control station. Let's take a look at each one of them:

- **Video Device**: As we saw in the Multicopter chapter, this is where you would specify a video capture device (hooked up to a video receiver) to display the video taken onboard the drone. Using the **Start** and **Stop** buttons starts and stops the video from being displayed behind the HUD on the Flight Data screen (in place of an artificial horizon).

- **Video Format**: This specifies the format for incoming video.

- **OSD Color**: This lets you set the color for all of the HUD items displayed.

- **Speech**: This enables the voice feedback functionality. This is where your ground control station calls out errors and mode changes using a text-to-speech engine.

- **UI Language**: This sets the language for the Mission Planner interface.

- **Joystick**: This activates the setup screen to utilize computer-based gaming joysticks to pilot your vehicle in place of a standard radio controller. This process is outlined in our Multicopter chapter.

- **Dist Units**: This sets the units of measurement for the Mission Planner interface (**Imperial**, **Metric**, and so on).

- **Speed Units**: This sets the units of measurement for the HUD during flight regarding speed (feet per second, meters per second, and so on).

This will not affect configuration units of measurement for speed. This is only for the real-time display of telemetry during vehicle use.

- **Telemetry Rates**: This is the rates at which telemetry readouts in Mission Planner are updated in simulation mode.
- **APM Reset**: This is a checkbox indicating whether or not APM is reset when a USB cable is plugged in. This is not a reset to the default parameters, but merely a hardware reboot.
- **Track Length**: This is the distance (in meters) that flight path which Pixhawk has travelled is displayed on the satellite map in the Flight Data screen.
- **Waypoints**: This shows whether or not the waypoints stored on the Pixhawk device are loaded into Mission Planner on connect.
- **HUD**: This is a checkbox indicating whether openGL is used (unchecked) or GDI+ is used (checked) to display the HUD information. If you don't know what these protocols are for display of layered visuals, just leave it unchecked (as most computers are compatible with openGL).
- **Map Follow**: This is a checkbox indicating whether the map stays with North pointed up on the screen (unchecked) or the map is rotated to match the orientation of the vehicle (checked).
- **Log Path**: This is the location on the computer where log files are saved.
- **Theme**: This is the color theme for the Mission Planner interface.
- **Layout**: This parameter is a key. By default, it is set to basic. By switching to advanced, you gain access to the **Advanced Params**, **Full Parameter List**, and **Full Parameter Tree** options in the Config/Tuning screen. You also gain access to the simulation and terminal Screens.
- **Additional buttons and checkboxes**: Almost confusingly under the **Layout** section are some additional parameters, which have nothing to do with layout. These are as follows:
    - **Start/Stop Vario**: This starts and stops the variometer features. Variometers are useful for gliders. They sense air pressure and altitude rates to measure the amount of lift the aircraft is experiencing. The net effect is making it easier for a glider pilot to find thermals to gain altitude with a glider.

- **AltitudeAngel:** This is especially useful in the US. **AltitudeAngel** will display an overlay on your map showing the restricted air space. This will help you stay out of trouble with the FAA, but should not be relied upon as your sole source. You should check FAA NOTAMS and sectional charts before every flight to make sure you are not violating any temporary restrictions, or other restricted airspace, which may not be documented in **AltitudeAngel**.

- **Password Protect Config**: This allows you to protect your configuration from changes by third parties via a password.

- **Show Airports**: This displays airports on your map.

- **ADSB**: ADSB is a protocol to recognize other aircraft and their vectors of travel. If you have an ADSB receiver, this enables the viewing of any aircraft in the area, which uses an ADSB transmitter. You should be aware that this is for receiver functionality only. Your drone will not appear on other aircraft's ADSB screens. For that, you would need an ADSB transmitter on your drone.

- **Opt Out Anon State**: 3D Robotics collects anonymous analytics of its Pixhawk modules. This checkbox opts out of transmitting your data to 3D Robotics.

- **Beta Updates**: When Mission Planner is booted up, this checkbox allows for Mission Planner to scan for updates, which are still in Beta testing. It is not advisable to download updates, which are not yet fully tested and released.

- **No RC Receiver**: This checkbox is to be checked if you are controlling via Mission Planner only (using the telemetry link and usually joysticks). It's always a good idea to have an RC receiver as backup even if you don't use it.

- **TFRs:** This will include the display of **Temporary Flight Restrictions** that 3D Robotics is aware of via the map view. Again, just as with **AltitudeAngel**, you should not rely on this as your sole source of information.

- **Mavlink Message Debug**: This shows a debug window having to do with Mavlink messages. This is highly useful if you are designing custom firmware for Pixhawk.

- **Testing Screen**: This is a very useful interface for troubleshooting Pixhawk. Here, you can export data, and at a glance check on features that are enabled/disabled. The following image shows the **Testing Screen**:

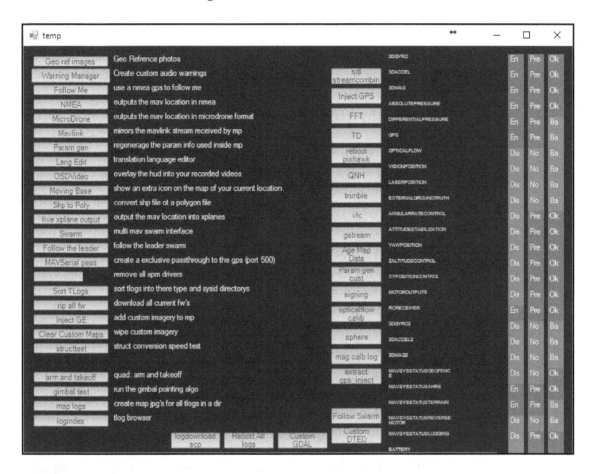

Flight Modes

This tab has the same functionality as the Flight Modes tab inside the Initial Setup screen. It allows you to set which flight modes are engaged when flipping the flight mode switch on your transmitter.

Basic Tuning

The **Basic Tuning** tab is where you can manually tune the flight characteristics of Pixhawk in modes, which require stabilization. Each axis (**Pitch**, **Roll**, and **Yaw**) is individually set with the following parameters:

- **Proportional Gain (P)**: This value is how much Pixhawk tries to correct to get the vehicle to the attitude it is supposed to be. For instance, how much elevator is applied to pitch the aircraft up to where it is supposed to be. Higher numbers make the craft more responsive or *twitchy*. Lower numbers make transitions smoother.

- **Integral Gain (I)**: You can think of this as an automatic trim adjustment. It takes in past discrepancies between the desired attitude and the actual attitude and corrects controls to account for this. Higher numbers mean more automatic trim, and lower numbers mean less.

- **Derivitive Gain (D)**: This one dampens how reactive the PI adjustments are. Numbers too high can damage servos and motors because they may begin to *flutter*.

- **INT_MAX**: This is the maximum value that can be used by **Integral Gain (I)**.

The other sections of this screen require a very in-depth explanation on their use. I believe Basic Tuning should be renamed to just Tuning. For this explanation, refer to `Chapter 7`, *The Holy Grail – A Fixed Wing Drone (Airplane)*, where we explain in great detail the tuning parameters on this screen.

Standard Params

The **Standard Params** screen is a long list of all of the basic parameters within Pixhawk which can be changed. Many of these parameters can be changed using the **graphic user interface** (**GUI**) on other screens within Mission Planner, or using the wizards. It is important though to note where to dive in and change the parameters manually. Here are all of the **Standard Params** and their functions:

- **ACRO_LOCKING**: Think of this as a **Panic** mode when operating an acrobatic aircraft in **ACRO** mode. If you let go of the sticks, the vehicle will level out and maintain altitude by engaging the **ALT HOLD** mode.

- **ACRO_PITCH_RATE**: This sets the maximum pitch rate in **ACRO** mode.

- **ACRO_ROLL_RATE**: This sets the maximum roll rate in **ACRO** mode.

- **ADSB_ENABLE**: This is not the same as the Planner ADSB. It actually facilitates an ADSB receiver mounted on the aircraft, which will automatically sense and avoid other aircraft which utilize the ADSB protocol. This is receiver only not a transmitter, so other aircraft will not see you on their ADSB displays.
- **AHRS_TRIM_X**: This compensates for the difference between the roll of the aircraft, and the roll angle of the Pixhawk's mounted roll angle. This is easily set using the **Calibrate Level** feature in the initial setup screen.
- **AHRS_TRIM_Y**: This is same as **AHRS_TRIM_X**, but works on the pitch axis.
- **ARMING_CHECK**: This is a series of checkboxes allowing you to specify which checks are performed in order to allow the vehicle to be armed. The default is **All**.
- **ARSPD_FBW_MAX**: This is the maximum airspeed allowed when using modes that utilize an automatic throttle feature (such as autopilot). It's very useful to keep from overstressing the airframe.
- **ARSPD_FBW_MIN**: This is the inverse of **ARSPD_FBW_MAX**; this sets the minimum airspeed to maintain in order to avoid stalls.
- **ARSPD_TYPE**: This is the type of sensor used to calculate airspeed (pitot tube).
- **ARSPD_USE**: This sets whether or not to use the airspeed sensor.
- **AUTOTUNE_LEVEL**: This sets how aggressive autotune is when tuning the aircraft. Higher numbers means the aircraft is more aggressive, resulting in greater responsiveness. However, adjusting this number could result in crashes due to exceeding aggressiveness than the airframe can handle, or being too sluggish to actually stabilize the aircraft with numbers too low.
- **BATT_CURR_PIN**: Very rarely used, this sets which pin the battery sensor is active on for measuring the current. Usually, setting this up using the basic GUI in the Initial Setup screen is most advisable.
- **BATT_MONITOR**: This sets how the voltage is measured by the battery sensor.
- **BATT_VOLT_PIN**: This is similar to **BATT_CURR_PIN**, but instead of measuring current, it measures the voltage.
- **BATT2_CURR_PIN**: This is the same as **BATT_CURR_PIN** for a second battery sensor.
- **BATT2_MONITOR**: This is the same as **BATT_MONITOR** for a second battery.
- **BATT2_VOLT_PIN**: This is the same as **BATT_VOLT_PIN** for a second battery.
- **BRD_SAFETYENABLE**: This facilitates the use of a safety arming switch (or button) on the vehicle to prearm Pixhawk.

- **CAM_FEEDBACK_PIN**: This facilitates the use of feedback from a camera (via a hotshoe connection), which will enter into the Pixhawk logs that a photo was successfully taken. This is highly useful for manually geotagging photos after they are taken using Pixhawk's GPS information. This parameter is the pin number to use for this feedback.

- **CAM_FEEDBACK_POL**: The polarity of the camera feedback. TriggerHigh is used to take a picture when the voltage escalates and TriggerLow is used to take a picture when the voltage drops.

- **CAM_RELAY_ON**: This is similar to **CAM_FEEDBACK_POL**, this sets when the camera relay has been activated by high or low voltage.

- **CAM_TRIGG_TYPE**: This specifies how Pixhawk would send a shutter trigger to the camera.

- **CAN_P1_DRIVER**: This activates the use of CAN buses on Pixhawk.

- **CAN_P2_DRIVER**: This activates a second CAN bus.

- **CHUTE_ENABLED**: This is used to check whether or not a parachute deployment system is present on the vehicle.

- **COMPASS_DEC**: This shows the difference between true North and Magnetic North. This is set by calibrating the compass automatically.

- **FBWB_CLIMB_RATE**: This sets how fast the vehicle will climb with elevators at full deflection in **FBWB** and **CRUISE** modes.

- **FBWB_ELEV_REV**: This is used to check whether the elevators are reversed in the **FBWB** mode (whether pushing forward on elevator control makes the aircraft rise or fall).

- **FENCE_ACTION**: This specifies the action to take when a geofence is breached.

- **FENCE_AUTOENABLE**: This sets whether a geofence is automatically put in place during automatic take off and removed during auto-landings.

- **FENCE_MAXALT**: This specifies the maximum altitude (in meters) an aircraft can fly when geofencing is enabled.

- **FENCE_MINALT**: This specifies the lowest altitude (in meters) an aircraft can fly when geofencing is enabled.

- **FENCE_RET_RALLY**: This sets how Pixhawk reacts to breaching a geofence (whether it returns to a rally point, home, or just to where the breach happened).

- **FENCE_RET_ALT**: This specifies the altitude that the aircraft returns from breaching the geofence at. A setting of 0 maintains the current altitude.

- **FLOW_ENABLE**: This is used to check whether or not optical flow sensors are used.

- **FLOW_FXSCALER**: This is used to account for lens length on an optical flow sensor. Increasing the number actually reduces the scale factor on the x axis.
- **FLOW_FYSCALER**: This is used to account for lens length on an optical flow sensor. Increasing the number actually reduces the scale factor on the y axis.
- **FLOW_ORIENT_YAW**: This sets the centi-degrees of variance between the aircraft and the yaw of the optical flow sensor.
- **FLTMODE(1-6)**: This sets what the flight modes are for different positions of the flight mode switch on the controller.
- **FS_GCS_ENABL**: This is used to check whether or not a failsafe state is activated upon loss of signal with the **ground control station** (**GCS**).
- **FS_LONG_ACTN**: This sets the action to be taken in the event of a long failsafe (see **FS_LONG_TIMEOUT**).
- **FS_LONG_TIMEOUT**: This is the number of seconds that a failsafe state exists before activating **FS_LONG_ACTN**.
- **FS_SHORT_ACTN**: This sets the action to be taken while waiting for **FS_LONG_TIMEOUT**.
- **FS_SHORT_TIMEOUT**: This is the number of seconds before the **FS_SHORT_ACTN** is activated in the event of a failsafe event. This is useful to prevent mode shifts during a small bit of signal interference, and so on.
- **GROUND_STEER_ALT**: This is the altitude (in meters), which the rudder control will also control a wheel servo to enable ground steering. A setting of 0 allows wheel control at all altitudes.
- **INVERTEDFLT_CH**: This specifies the controller channel, which will enable inverted flight capabilities.
- **LAND_TYPE**: This specifies the type of landing to execute during auto-landing. (Standard versus Deep Tail).
- **LIM_PITCH_MAX**: This is the maximum pitch angle during stabilized flight modes.
- **LIM_PITCH_MIN**: This limits the angle at which the nose can be pointed down during stabilized flight modes.
- **LIM_ROLL_CD**: This is the maximum roll angle (in centi-degrees) of a roll in either direction.
- **LOG_BACKEND_TYPE**: This specifies how logs are stored (File, mavLink, or both).
- **LOG_DISARMED**: This specifies whether the logs are created while in a disarmed state (as well as armed).
- **LOG_FILE_DSRMOT**: This dictates whether the current log file is closed when the vehicle is disarmed.

- **LOG_REPLAY**: This specifies whether the necessary log information is written to a log file for replay.
- **MAG_ENABLE**: This sets whether or not the compass is used.
- **MNT_ANGMAX_PAN**: This sets the maximum pan angle of a gimbal mount.
- **MNT_ANGMAX_ROL**: This sets the maximum roll angle of a gimbal mount.
- **MNT_ANGMAX_TIL**: This sets the maximum tilt angle of a gimbal mount.
- **MNT_ANGMIN_PAN**: This sets the minimum pan angle of a gimbal mount.
- **MNT_ANGMIN_ROL**: This sets the minimum roll angle of a gimbal mount.
- **MNT_ANGMIN_TIL**: This sets the minimum tilt angle of a gimbal mount.
- **MNT_DEFLT_MODE**: This sets the default mode of the gimbal mount.
- **MNT_STICK_SPD**: This is used to determine how fast the gimbal moves when user input is given (how sensitive it is).
- **MNT_LEAD_PTCH**: This sets the sensitivity of a gimbal mount to pitching of an aircraft. Larger numbers make it compensate more. This number should be increased enough to make the mount responsive, but not to overcompensate.
- **MNT_LEAD_RLL**: This is the same as **MNT_LEAD_PTCH**, but on the roll axis.
- **MNT_NEUTRAL_X**: This is the home position of the mount's roll axis (level).
- **MNT_NEUTRAL_Y**: This is the home position of the tilt axis of the gimbal mount (level).
- **MNT_NEUTRAL_Z**: This is the home yaw position of the gimbal mount (straight ahead).
- **MNT_RC_IN_PAN**: This is the RC channel used to control the pan axis of a gimbal.
- **MNT_RC_IN_ROLL**: This is the RC channel used to control the roll axis of a gimbal.
- **MNT_RC_IN_TILT**: This is the RC channel used to control the tilt axis of a gimbal.
- **MNT_RETRACT_X**: This is the angle on the roll axis to set the camera at on a gimbal if you have a retractable gimbal, and the gimbal is retracted.
- **MNT_RETRACT_Y**: This is the angle on the pitch axis to set the camera at on a gimbal if you have a retractable gimbal, and the gimbal is retracted.
- **MNT_RETRACT_Z**: This is the angle on the pan axis to set the camera at on a gimbal if you have a retractable gimbal, and the gimbal is retracted.
- **MNT_STAB_PAN**: This is used to check whether or not to stabilize the pan axis of a gimbal.
- **MNT_STAB_ROLL**: This is used to check whether or not to stabilize the roll axis of a gimbal.

- **MNT_STAB_TILT**: This is used to check whether or not to stabilize the pitch axis of a gimbal.
- **MNT_TYPE**: This sets the type of gimbal mount (none, servo, and mavLink).
- **NAV_CONTROLLER**: This is to enable the use of experimental navigation controller. L1 is the default here.
- **NAVL1_PERIOD**: This sets the turning radius (in meters) during autonomous flight.
- **Q_ENABLE**: This enables the quadplane (hybrid) features of Pixhawk.
- **RALLY_INCL_HOME**: This checks whether the home point is a safe place to land during RTL.
- **RELAY_DEFAULT**: This sets the state of the camera relay upon boot of Pixhawk.
- **RELAY_PIN(1,2,3,4)**: This sets the pin number for relay control of a camera.
- **RNGFND_ADDR**: This is specific to the LightWare I2C lidar rangefinder. It allows for the use of multiple rangefinders on different addresses.
- **RNGFND_FUNCTION**: This sets how the rangefinder's feedback is interpreted (linear, inverted, and hyperbolic).
- **RNGFND_GNDCLEAR**: This is used to determine how far a downward-facing rangefinder is from the ground when an aircraft has landed.
- **RNGFND_LANDING**: This is used to check whether or not to use the rangefinder to assist with landings.
- **RNGFND_PIN**: This is the pin used for analog (non-I2C) rangefinders.
- **RNGFND_RMETRIC**: This is used to set whether or not an analog rangefinder is ratiometric (most are).
- **RNGFND_STOP_PIN**: This sets the pin used for an analog rangefinder's measurement.
- **RNGFND_TYPE**: This sets the type of rangefinder implemented.
- **RPM_PIN**: This is the pin to be used for a motor RPM sensor.
- **RPM_TYPE**: This is the type of RPM sensor implemented.
- **RPM2_PIN**: This allows for the use of a second RPM sensor and specifies the pin that is used for it.
- **RSSI_ANA_PIN**: This specifies the pin number for an analog RSSI (Received Signal Strength Indicator) module.
- **RSSI_PIN_HIGH**: This sets the maximum voltage for an RSSI module's output when the signal strength is high.
- **RSSI_PIN_LOW**: This sets the minimum voltage when an RSSI module's signal strength is low.
- **RSSI_TYPE**: This is the type of RSSI module.

- **RTL_AUTOLAND**: This is used to set whether or not to execute an autonomous landing when RTL is engaged.
- **RTL_RADIUS**: This is the radius to loiter around the home point when RTL is engaged.
- **RUDD_DT_GAIN**: This the ratio of the rudder to differential thrust. Differential thrust is used on multiengine aircraft (for example, when executing a left turn, the left motor will spin down slightly, and the right motor will spin up to help yaw the aircraft).
- **SERIAL(0-5)_BAUD**: This is the rate of data transfer on the specified serial bus.
- **SERIAL(0-5)_PROTOCOL**: This is used to determine what protocol is used on the specified serial bus (mavLink, and so on.)
- **SERVO(1-16)_FUNCTION**: This specifies what this servo port will control.
- **SERVO(1-16)_MAX**: This is the maximum value (PWM) the servo can receive on this channel.
- **SERVO(1-16)_MIN**: This is the minimum value (PWM) the servo can receive on this channel.
- **SERVO(1-16)_REVERSED**: This is used to set whether or not the servo values are to be inverted on this channel.
- **SERVO(1-16)_TRIM**: This is used to set the trim for the servo on this channel. Use this in place of using the trim functionality on your controller.
- **STALL_PREVENTION**: This is used to enable or disable stall prevention. An airspeed sensor (pitot) is required for this feature.
- **TECS_CLIMB_MAX**: This is the maximum climb rate (in meters per second) an aircraft can climb at **THR_MAX** (while maintaining airspeed).
- **TECS_SINK_MIN**: This is the maximum sink rate of an aircraft while throttle is set to **THR_MIN** and the aircraft does not accelerate beyond the **CLIMB_MAX** speed.
- **TELEM_DELAY**: This is the number of seconds to wait after Pixhawk boots up to begin sending telemetry data.
- **TERRAIN_FOLLOW**: This enables the ability of Pixhawk to follow the altitude of the terrain below it during autonomous flight modes. You should have the ground control station connected to enable this feature. It uses terrain data to calculate altitude rather than merely using altitude in relation to the home point.
- **THR_FAILSAFE**: This enables/disables the functionality of activating a failsafe even if the throttle drops below a specific value. It's a good way of testing for a receiver signal from the radio transmitter. For instance, if your transmitter's minimum throttle is a PWM value of 980, upon disconnect the throttle may drop to 0. So, setting a value of 950 would be good.

- **THR_MAX**: This is the maximum throttle that Pixhawk can apply to the motor (in percentage).
- **THR_MIN**: This is the minimum throttle for Pixhawk to apply to the motor. For autonomous landings, you'll want to set this to 0. For ESCs that allow for reverse thrust, you may set this to a negative value to act as a brake.
- **THR_SLEWRATE**: This is the maximum amount of change per second. This will make throttle transitions more smooth. Be careful though, as setting this value too low may result in a stall.
- **THROTTLE_NUDGE**: This allows the pilot to nudge the throttle up or down when in automatic throttle flight modes.
- **TRIM_AUTO**: This enables Pixhawk to automatically adjust trim values for controls surfaces when not in the manual mode.
- **TRIM_THROTTLE**: This is the throttle to be applied (in percentage) during normal flight.
- **TUNE_CHAN**: This enables the ability to tune PIDs using a knob or slider on your transmitter (value specifies the channel).
- **TUNE_MODE_REVERT**: This enables or disables Pixhawk reverting to previously saved tuning settings on a mode change. During tuning, changes are saved every 10 seconds. So, you'll have 10 seconds to revert by changing the modes.
- **TUNE_PARAM**: This sets which parameter is tuned using the **TUNE_CHAN** functionality.
- **TUNE_SELECTOR**: This is the switch channel on your remote, which will enable the **TUNE_CHAN** functionality.
- **WP_LOITER_RADIUS**: This sets the radius (in meters) around a waypoint to circle during **LOITER**. If set to a negative number, the orbit will be counter-clockwise.
- **WP_MAX_RADIUS**: This overrides the waypoint radius set in the Flight Plan Screen with a new value that dictates the radius from a waypoint for it to be considered completed. A value of 0 offers no override at all and leaves the waypoint radius of a mission intact.
- **WP_RADIUS**: This is similar to **WP_MAX_RADIUS** with no override. This is to avoid endlessly circling a waypoint, which has a radius too small for the aircraft to meet.

Advanced Params

These parameters should only be used by advanced users of Pixhawk who know exactly what they are doing. This is not a section to be experimented with. It controls the core functionality of Pixhawk and is very technical. They are also different between copter, plane, and rover models. For a complete list of the parameters and their functionality, visit the following web page; it is consistently updated with the latest parameters and options: http://ardupilot.org/copter/docs/parameters.html.

Full Parameter List

This section shows all parameters (standard and advanced), and their settings (raw data, which is usually numerical values, not plain text) as well as the options available, and a description of each. This is laid out in a table format.

Full Parameter Tree

Similar to the **Full Parameter List**, this tree offers a representation not only of the parameters in the list, but their relationship to each other.

The Simulation Screen

This screen allows the user to simulate autonomous flights based on their vehicle's settings to see how it would execute missions. It's also a great way to get familiar with flying Pixhawk while using the Mission Planner.

Mission Planner terminal

This is a **command line interface (CLI)** for Pixhawk. We'll only cover it briefly as Ardupilot.org indicates that it will be deprecated (phased out) of existence soon—and probably by the time you read this book. This is an area where you can literally test scripts you write for Pixhawk to execute by manually coding them. A full list of commands, and how to use this interface is available here:

http://ardupilot.org/dev/docs/using-the-command-line-interface.html.

Summary

In this chapter, we reviewed many of the interface components of Mission Planner. We also covered some features we haven't mentioned before. It's important to note that this chapter is meant mainly as a reference for your future use in your adventures developing prototypes using Pixhawk.

It's our sincere hope that you learned about Pixhawk, and prototype design built around it, as well as the fabrication of prototypes and bringing your ideas to life. We hope you enjoyed this book as much as we enjoyed writing it. Thank you for reading it, and you should congratulate yourself. It's an awful lot of information to consume!

Index

V

W

www.ingramcontent.com/pod-product-compliance
Lightning Source LLC
Chambersburg PA
CBHW080633060326
40690CB00021B/4916